os F^x

# Salsa & Merengue

## The Essential Step-by-Step Guide

# PAUL HARRIS

### With
## JANE YOUNG
RESEARCH AND COMPILATION ASSISTANT

√o3

SIGMA

**Published by** Sigma Leisure – an imprint of
Sigma Press, 1 South Oak Lane, Wilmslow, Cheshire SK9 6AR, England.

**British Library Cataloguing in Publication Data**
A CIP record for this book is available from the British Library.


**ISBN:** 1-85058-699-3


**Illustrations by:** My Hoang

**Cover artwork:** Stuart Fox

**Cover Design:** The Agency, Wilmslow


**Printed by:** MFP Design and Print

# Foreword

With this book, Paul Harris has produced an outstanding guide to the world of Salsa Music and Dance. Meticulously and accurately researched, yet easy to read, it gives a remarkable insight into every aspect of Salsa from the origins of the music to the structure of the dance, both clarifying and correcting commonly held misconceptions. *Salsa and Merengue, The Essential Step-by-Step Guide* is a major accomplishment – anyone who wants to know what Salsa Music and Dance is really about should consult this book. Newcomers and experts alike will not find a more authentic, enlightening and instructive source of reference.

## Nelson Batista (Cuba)
### *Salsa Dance Instructor and Examiner*

# Preface

Social dancing is one of the most popular pastimes in the world. Argentine Tango, Modern Jive and, most of all, Salsa all have their own "scenes" and are as fashionable today as any dances have ever been.

In the past, venues for couple dancing were mainly hotels and dance halls, now they are clubs. Owing to the massive interest in contemporary Latin-American dancing amongst younger social dancers, the United Kingdom Alliance, one of the world's leading professional dance teaching bodies and a corporate member of The British Dance Council, has formed a Club Dance Division adopting my own technique book on Merengue and Salsa as their syllabus for both amateur medal tests and professional examinations.

The dance style in Latin clubs today has moved dancers closer together again and Merengue and Salsa are undoubtedly the most popular dances. A few more experienced dancers may know the American style Mambo and the Cha Cha Cha. It is these dances, together with Argentine Tango, that one needs to know to be equipped for Latin-American social dancing today.

Research for this book has involved visits to the Dominican Republic, Cuba and several other Caribbean islands. These visits have combined with an extensive study of Latin-American music, political history and culture along with the assessment and consideration of several dance forms, including Afro-Cuban Jazz, Cuban Folkloric Dance, International, American and Club Style Latin-American dancing and Classical Ballet.

This book is designed as a step-by-step guide for all Salseros, both social dancers and teachers alike who have a passion for Salsa and enjoy dancing together – Latino style!

*Paul Harris*

# CONTENTS

## Introduction

## The Dances

## An Introduction to other Latin Rhythms

# *Essential Information*

# Why this book was written

As a dancer, choreographer and teacher in Central London I am very aware that Latin social dancing has an enormous following and is something one does today, in a Club. At the time of writing, almost all Salsa clubs run classes. Even though there are still some differences in what is taught, the contemporary style of both Merengue and Salsa has settled onto fairly common ground and this book aims to equip social dancers from beginner to advanced with the necessary steps and styling to enjoy dancing in Salsa clubs anywhere in the world.

In researching this book I have read most Social Dance technique books written since 1930. There has been a marked drop over the years in the amount of book space given to the principles of movement. It is also common for people embarking on learning to dance socially to have complicated variations thrown at them before they have mastered any ease of movement whatsoever. It makes all of the figures more simple to understand if posture, balance, timing, characterisation and preparation for movement are considered first. It need only be a few minutes but I believe that time spent on these fundamental principles when beginning is time well spent. I have therefore included some basic instruction on these issues before the step descriptions. If the reader is also attending dance classes this book can be used in conjunction with their instruction.

It is also my belief that a real understanding of the principles of movement is the most important aspect for any teacher of dancing to know, and Salsa teachers using this book as a guide should remember that learning to dance is not just about steps – steps are simply increasingly difficult ways of displaying the indigenous characteristic action of the given dance.

*Paul Harris*

# The Author

Paul Harris has had two enormously successful careers – in Dancing and Acting. As a Junior ballroom dancer, Paul was British, United Kingdom and International Champion in both Latin-American and Ballroom dancing and undisputed World No 1. As an amateur, he was the UK and West European Latin-American Champion. As a professional, Paul specialised in Exhibition/Theatre Arts, winning the British Professional title, and appeared in cabaret in many of the world's leading venues, including the Royal Albert Hall and the QE2.

Paul then studied acting at The Academy of Live and Recorded Arts (ALRA) along with jazz, ballet, tap and historical dance. Although he performed leading roles in productions of three West End dramas, his dance background was inescapable and he spent a year as A-Rab in the highly acclaimed 1988 revival of West Side Story with the breathtaking original Jerome Robbins choreography.

Paul's two careers inevitably came full circle when he was asked to form the London Theatre of Ballroom for the re-opening of the world famous Café de Paris, now once again one of London's leading exclusive night spots. London Theatre of Ballroom enjoyed a critically acclaimed six month run at the Café de Paris, making them the first dance-theatre company based on ballroom dancing ever to have such a long season in the West End. London Theatre of Ballroom has now become one of Britain's leading dance companies and is much in demand for cabaret. This successful blend has lead to Paul being one of the world's leading experts in his field, working at the highest levels in film, TV and theatre, choreographing dance scenes that require an accurate re-creation of social dancing and a genuine understanding of acting.

Paul has coached some of the most famous actors in the world, including Sean Connery, and he has worked with the Oscar nominated director, John Amiel. He is the resident social dance coach at the prestigious Actors Centre in London and choreographs show work for leading dance couples. Paul is also the author of the first technique book to be recognised by a professional dance teaching body for Salsa, bringing club-style Latin social dancing into the dance industry.

# The Music

The word "Salsa" literally means "sauce" but the origin of the term Salsa in the dance world is the cause of much debate amongst experts. It is, however, generally accepted by musicians that Salsa is the generic term for a musical fusion of Cuban rhythms and hot, spicy American "front line" instrumentation, creating a sound that might be described as having sauce and savour – "salsa y sabor".

The elements contained in the melting pot of Salsa can be traced back as far as the researcher wishes to go. The "call and response" vocal style is undoubtedly West African, many elements of Salsa have definite Spanish roots and the Cha Cha Cha, which can be played salsa style or not, is reputed to have a Country Dance/Contradanza/Danzon progression. What is beyond question is that Enrique Jorrin, a Danzon composer and violinist, has official recognition from the Cuban government as being the "creator" of the Cha Cha Cha for his 1948 composition, "La Engañadora". It is also worth noting that the Cha Cha Cha is played extensively in the USA and is covered by most US Salsa bands.

Almost all of the rhythms (of which there are many) played by authentic Salsa bands existed in Cuba prior to the revolution. Rhythms such as Son, Guajira, Bolero, Guaracha, Mambo, Cha Cha Cha and the Rumba complex (Yambu, Guaguancó and Columbia) were already standard fare in pre-Castro Cuba. It was the subsequent fleeing to the USA of artists and musicians from the new regime and the inevitable musical experimentation that lead to a 1960s/70s boom in the new Hispanic populated areas of America's main cities creating a new and exciting sound – Salsa. Out of this came a group of artists recording on the "Fania" label who were dedicated to preserving and progressing their heritage. Tito Puente, Celia Cruz, Johnny Pacheco, Machito, Ruben Blades, Ray Barretto, Eddie Palmieri and Willie Colón were among the leaders. Some recorded together as the Fania All Stars.

Cuban bands remaining and recording in their homeland, such as Orchestra Aragón took longer to encompass the American influence and for many years continued to record in the authentic Cuban style. Indeed, music can still be found in Cuba today recorded in the manner of the old Cuban Charangas with a front line of violins and flutes rather than with salsa style brass.

Latin-American musical forms that have spawned dance crazes are generally the result of hundreds of years of cultural evolution. Salsa is no exception and is currently undergoing yet more fusion as it spreads more and more to Europe, encompassing Colombian, Puerto Rican and other Afro-Caribbean musical elements. Bands are now regularly playing Merengue, a dance from the Dominican Republic with a heritage quite different from other Salsa rhythms. This is possibly because its basic step pattern has a simpler construction and can be picked up and enjoyed more easily by non-Latinos.

Mainstream Latin-American music has, of course, been popular since Don Azpiazou's Havana Casino Orchestra took New York by storm in 1930 with "The Peanut Vendor", spawning the Hollywood Rumba Rage. However, at the time of writing, Salsa clubs in the United Kingdom are enjoying unprecedented popularity. In addition to some 25 Salsa clubs in London, there are clubs in Edinburgh, Glasgow, Aberdeen, Oxford, Brighton, Blackpool, Newcastle, Windsor, Birmingham, Cambridge, Leeds, Liverpool, St Albans, Manchester, Nottingham, Reading and Sheffield, and new clubs are opening up all the time.

It is common for clubs to have live music on a regular basis with most bands playing Salsa and Merengue. Tango Salons are usually held separately, although enormous Latin-American music and dance events are occasionally held under the same roof.

Unlike regular nightclubs, most people go to Latin clubs simply because they enjoy dancing in couples and because they love the music – Salsa!

**N.B.** It is worth noting that, even though they are not covered in this book due to more limited popularity, there are clubs where Lambada and Cumbia are danced.

> *Music for Merengue and Salsa can be found in the World Music section of any major music store*

# TECHNIQUE

## HOW TO STAND

For all dancing, an understanding of posture is important. A professional dancer will spend many hours improving their stance. For social dance, a simple understanding of the correct carriage of the weight of the body in order to obtain good balance will make the whole process of learning to dance more enjoyable and, indeed, is essential if one is to enjoy dancing in close contact hold with another person.

Both man and lady, at whatever level they are at, should have an understanding of their own posture and balance and know how to create a dynamic between them in order to make dancing together an enjoyable experience from the beginning.

To obtain good posture and balance the spine should be aligned and the "centre" line of the body pitched slightly over the balls of the feet between the three points of balance, the big and little toes and the heel. It is a physical fact that when moving forwards, unless consciously decided otherwise, the "centre" will go first and the leg will arrive to catch the weight. When moving backwards a base is created for the weight to move on to. A simple exercise of examining walking forwards and backwards can help understand this and possibly prevent bad habits from the start. It is important that dancers of all levels are able to move their body weight effortlessly if they are to enjoy their dancing. The body should be toned through the torso, and this tone should be felt by both dancers at the "centre", even if the only point of contact is the hand.

It is quite possible that readers of this book have already tried aerobics, Alexander technique or that they go to a gym. Therefore, it will come as no surprise to hear that there is a process to go through before embarking on any dance steps and, even if it is only for a short time, how to stand is stage one.

**N.B.** The principle of the movement of the "centre" as being responsible for body motion was first notated by Beauchamp in 1704!

## THE HOLDS

Having attained good posture, the upper body should be held with a proud, toned, erect poise with the man's left hand and the lady's right hand held relatively high at eye level. In some styles, the hands are even above the head. The man's right hand folds neatly around the lady's waist and the lady's left hand folds around the man's back, neck or upper right arm (shoulder blade) when in close contact hold. In this hold, the lady is offset slightly to the man's right side so that the man's right foot is between the lady's feet. If this position is maintained it will assist all rotational movement when in close contact.

When in close or open hold the distance between the couple can vary and open hold may consist of left hand to right, right hand to left, left hand to left, right hand to right or double hold. There are, generally, three ways of holding hands: a) the regular method where the lady's hand is placed in the man's hand; b) the man may hold the lady's hand, palm to palm; and c) occasionally, the man may hold the lady's wrist.

*Close contact hold*

If one or both arms are free, they should be held in an unaffected and very natural way.

# MOVING WEIGHT OVER TIME

The dances and steps in this book increase progressively in degree of timing difficulty. If the somewhat simple timing of the Merengue is understood first then Salsa, which has only three steps in a four beat bar, will be easier to learn. The indigenous hip action of the club style Latin dances has been known for many years in the USA as Cuban Motion, and Cuban Motion is integral to the timing of each dance as a hip movement can account for beats or half beats not covered by steps.

This book uses the accepted form of counting rhythm, i.e. slows and quicks, but the steps are structured into two, four or eight bar combinations for learning purposes. Although, of course, most social dancers in clubs will not adhere to this, good social dancers will subconsciously use the *cadencia* (phrasing) of the music and it is an excellent device to attune the ears to musical structure.

# CHARACTERISATION - CUBAN MOTION

The musical elements of the dances referred to in this book are broadly African-Spanish and the dancing should reflect that.

Having created a proud, very elegant stance, the hips move separately from the upper body in opposition to the step being taken at any one time. The action is lateral and understated – less is more! As pressure is taken on the inside edge of the ball of the stepping foot onto a flexed knee, the hip moves freely in the opposite direction, eg step left, hip to right. It is not necessary to fully straighten the legs to achieve an easy hip swing. Any jazz class will prove beyond doubt that full movement of the hips can be achieved whilst in second position plié!

It is also vital that to be equipped for Club Latin dancing, no affectations in the lower body are apparent. Club style Latin dancing appears easy, casual and sexy and the opposition hip action is all!

## SEEING THE PATTERN

Once one begins to learn the steps, it is desirable to have a clear picture of the step pattern individually. If pushed or guided through steps without being able to "see the pattern" it will take far longer for a man to be able to lead a step and a woman to follow. Also, in order to dance well with another person one should understand what one is doing oneself. When posture, timing, Cuban Motion and a mental picture of the basic patterns are understood it is easier and quicker to progress.

The step patterns in this book increase progressively in degree of difficulty and have been structured with a tried and tested progressive learning process in mind. As with everything, begin at the beginning and remember, technique is the greatest freedom.

## LEADING AND FOLLOWING

Being able to send and receive signals from and to the "centre" is the single most important aspect in indicating and following a movement. Having understood the tone of the body, this tone should continue through the arms without tension in the wrists.

A sound understanding of the dynamic required will enable leads to be given without force and will also enable the lady to recognise leads more easily. It will ultimately result in leading and following being far less aggressive than is often experienced with the usual pushing and pulling that goes on under the guise of leading and following!

Every movement one makes requires a preparatory movement, therefore the person leading the step should indicate on at least the beat before.

If the techniques described above are followed the process of learning to lead and follow will be easier and can almost become visually indicational, only requiring a very light touch indeed.

# TERMINOLOGY

## TERMS

All dances that are covered by the umbrella of Social Dancing were at some time not standardised. They all evolved from dances used in social environments and were subsequently subject to standardisation in order that they may correctly be taught and passed on by dance teachers. Merengue and Salsa are no exception. It is for this reason that whilst retaining the greatest respect for the wonderful improvisational skills of many club dancers, the accepted terms of the world of social dance are used in this book. Therefore, the following terms are explained:

**Tempo** - Denotes the speed at which the music is played

**Rhythm** - Is a regular occurrence of an accented beat or beats in the music. Sometimes referred to as individual expression. In teaching dancing it is often counted in slows and quicks.

**Timing** - The numerical count to describe the musical value of steps. In teaching dancing timing refers to the ability of the dancer to correspond movement with music.

**Promenade Position** - A slight opening of the man's left and lady's right sides in order to step forward and across in the same direction.

**Opening Out Position** - A backward step making up to half a turn

**Right Side-By-Side Position** - Lady on man's right side, both facing the same direction

**Left Side-By-Side Position** - Lady on man's left side, both facing the same direction

# ABBREVIATIONS

| | | |
|---|---|---|
| **R** | - | Right |
| **RF** | - | Right Foot |
| **L** | - | Left |
| **LF** | - | Left Foot |
| **PP** | - | Promenade Position |
| **FW** | - | Footwork |
| **S** | - | A "Slow" step (2 beats of music) |
| **Q** | - | A "Quick" step (1 beat of music) |
| **½** | - | ½ a "Quick" step (½ a beat of music) |

# STEP NAMES

Currently step names may still vary from club to club, and sometimes from country to country, so names are used that are internationally known, or that are descriptive of the step. If a step is known by more than one name it is cross-referenced where possible. All step names in this book have been recognised and adopted as the official step names for Merengue and Salsa by the United Kingdom Alliance of Professional Teachers of Dancing, who are corporate members of The British Dance Council.

# STEP STRUCTURE

It is common for social dance technique books to describe steps in isolation. For both teaching and learning purposes I have found it beneficial to structure steps within two, four or eight bar combinations, which is a very good way to understand how and where a step may be used. Most people have no problem in linking figures together once steps have been learned. Therefore, precedes and follows to particular steps have simply been suggested in this book in order to allow for flexibility in linking moves together.

# The Progressive Method of Learning

The suggested progression of steps is based on an extensive study of a physical learning process. As in any other dance form it is essential that for quick learning each step is progressive in degree of difficulty. Many people simply want to be basically equipped to dance in clubs. Therefore, the steps suggested for **Level 1** do precisely that and, if properly understood, are adequate preparation for basic Club style dancing. The **Level 2** moves offer a more detailed, structured understanding of partnering, and once progressing to **Level 3**, some combinations have been suggested as guidelines. However, it should be noted that once spotted as a good social dancer in a Club, women especially should be prepared to follow any combination of turns!

---

*LEVEL 1 - BEGINNER*        *STEPS 1 - 5*

*LEVEL 2 - INTERMEDIATE*        *STEPS 6 - 10*

*LEVEL 3 -ADVANCED*        *STEPS 11 - 15*

---

**N.B.** Any Salsa teachers using this book as a guide should note that the steps in both dances in this book correspond with the recommended syllabus of the United Kingdom Alliance of Professional Teachers of Dancing, as follows:

*Level 1 is from the Intro Award syllabus.*
*Level 2 is from the Bronze Medal syllabus.*
*Level 3 is from the Silver and Gold Medal syllabuses.*

Improvised routines are required for awards above Gold.

# Salsa & Merengue

## The Dances

# MERENGUE

**Time signature:** 2/4 time.   **Tempo:** 55 – 70 bpm.   **FW:** ball flat throughout.

Merengue is a dance generally considered to be from the Dominican Republic, although some claim that it has its origins in Haiti. It has been a standardised Latin dance in the American style since the 1950s. The figures used in today's club style Merengue differ from the ballroom version in that it is very much a spot dance not moving along the line of dance and the style of both the music and the dance shows a more earthy and sensual approach using close, intricate rotational movements.

In Merengue there are no "two beat" steps, i.e. slows – one step is taken to each beat of the music.

In the early days of the Merengue's appearance in ballroom dancing, the "Lame Duck" styling was often used but has now become unfashionable and is not danced in Latin clubs today. In the ballroom version, the Merengue travels progressively around the line of dance (anticlockwise).

The Merengue steps in this book are merely a strong guide to the steps most commonly used and it should be noted that improvisation is common and many combinations of steps are danced.

The action used throughout club style Merengue is Cuban Motion (see introductory section of this book) which is relatively easy to master in this dance.

---

*IN MERENGUE, CUBAN MOTION IS NOT SIMPLY A MATTER OF STYLING, IT IS ESSENTIAL THAT EVERY STEP IS TAKEN WITH DELAYED HIP ACTION AS IT IS INTEGRAL TO THE TIMING.*

---

# MERENGUE

## LEVEL 1 - BEGINNER

1   *The Basic Movement*

2   *Progressive Basics (Forwards and Backwards)*

3   *Rock Basic*

4   *Separations*

5   *Parallel Walkaround (Left & Right)*

## LEVEL 2 - INTERMEDIATE

6   *Underarm Turn Right*

7   *Underarm Turn Left*

8   *Armlock Turn and Walkaround*

9   *Wrap and Walkaround*

10  *Opposition Walkaround*

## LEVEL 3 - ADVANCED

11  *Natural Top*

12  *Hand Change Turn*

13  *Merengue Circle*

14  *Arm Breaker*

15  *Rolling Off The Arm*

# 1 THE BASIC MOVEMENT

The Basic Movement amounts to a lateral hip swing, stepping in place, transferring weight alternately from foot to foot using Cuban Motion. It is usually danced in close contact hold, sometimes in double hold, for example, following a separation, and occasionally apart with the embellishment of a shimmy. When in close contact hold turn to L or R is often used.

Start with the man's weight on RF (hip to right) and the lady's weight on LF (hip to left) feet slightly apart, in close contact hold. **Cuban Motion is used throughout.**

## MAN

| Step | Description | Rhythm | Beat |
|------|-------------|--------|------|
| 1 | LF step in place, transfer weight to LF | Q | 1 |
| 2 | RF step in place, transfer weight to RF | Q | 2 |
| 3 | LF step in place, transfer weight to LF | Q | 1 |
| 4 | RF step in place, transfer weight to RF | Q | 2 |
| 5-8 | Repeat steps 1-4 | Q's | 1,2,1,2 |
| | | | 4 bars |

## LADY

| Step | Description | Rhythm | Beat |
|------|-------------|--------|------|
| 1 | RF step in place, transfer weight to RF | Q | 1 |
| 2 | LF step in place, transfer weight to LF | Q | 2 |
| 3 | RF step in place, transfer weight to RF | Q | 1 |
| 4 | LF step in place, transfer weight to LF | Q | 2 |
| 5-8 | Repeat steps 1-4 | Q's | 1,2,1,2 |
| | | | 4 bars |

The Basic Movement can be repeated or linked as required and is usually danced with turn to the right. When the turn becomes very tight the feet may cross in front or behind developing into the Natural Top. However, the Basic Movement is best initially learned in place without turn to establish Cuban Motion. The Basic Movement may be danced gradually getting lower and lower focusing the movement more into the hip action rather than the step.

## 2   PROGRESSIVE BASICS (FORWARDS & BACKWARDS)

Progressive Basics (Forwards and Backwards) are usually danced in close contact hold or double hold and can be danced with or without turn to L or R.

Start with the man's weight on RF (hip to right) and the lady's weight on LF (hip to left) feet slightly apart, in close contact hold. **Cuban Motion is used throughout.**

## MAN

| Step | Description | Rhythm | Beat |
|------|-------------|--------|------|
| 1 | LF forward | Q | 1 |
| 2 | RF forward passing LF | Q | 2 |
| 3 | LF forward passing RF | Q | 1 |
| 4 | RF forward passing LF (small step) | Q | 2 |
| 5 | Replace weight to LF | Q | 1 |
| 6 | RF back passing LF | Q | 2 |
| 7 | LF back passing RF | Q | 1 |
| 8 | RF to side | Q | 2 |
| | | | 4 bars |

## LADY

| Step | Description | Rhythm | Beat |
|------|-------------|--------|------|
| 1 | RF back | Q | 1 |
| 2 | LF back passing RF | Q | 2 |
| 3 | RF back passing LF | Q | 1 |
| 4 | LF back passing RF (small step) | Q | 2 |
| 5 | Replace weight to RF | Q | 1 |
| 6 | LF forward passing RF | Q | 2 |
| 7 | RF forward passing LF | Q | 1 |
| 8 | LF to side | Q | 2 |
| | | | 4 bars |

Progressive Basics are a development of the Basic Movement and can be repeated or linked as required.

# 3    ROCK BASIC

The Rock Basic is usually danced in close contact hold.

Start with the man's weight on RF (hip to right) and the lady's weight on LF (hip to left) feet slightly apart, in close contact hold.

**Cuban Motion is used throughout.**

## MAN

| Step | Description | Rhythm | Beat |
|------|-------------|--------|------|
| 1 | LF forward, transfer weight | Q | 1 |
| 2 | Replace weight to RF | Q | 2 |
| 3 | LF back passing RF, transfer weight to LF | Q | 1 |
| 4 | Replace weight to RF | Q | 2 |
| 5-8 | Repeat steps 1-4 | Q's | 1,2,1,2 |
|  |  |  | 4 bars |

## LADY

| Step | Description | Rhythm | Beat |
|------|-------------|--------|------|
| 1 | RF back, transfer weight | Q | 1 |
| 2 | Replace weight to LF | Q | 2 |
| 3 | RF forward passing LF, transfer weight to RF | Q | 1 |
| 4 | Replace weight to LF | Q | 2 |
| 5-8 | Repeat steps 1-4 | Q's | 1,2,1,2 |
|  |  |  | 4 bars |

Rock Basics are sometimes taught as the first step in Merengue and can be repeated or linked as required.

# 4    SEPARATIONS

Separations are usually danced in close contact hold or double hold and, as the name implies, is a movement where both dancers progress backwards and forwards away from and towards each other retaining double hold.

Start with the man's weight on RF (hip to right) and the lady's weight on LF (hip to left) feet slightly apart, in close contact or double hold.

**Cuban Motion is used throughout.**

## MAN

| Step | Description | Rhythm | Beat |
|------|-------------|--------|------|
| 1 | LF back | Q | 1 |
| 2 | RF back passing LF | Q | 2 |
| 3 | LF back passing RF | Q | 1 |
| 4 | RF back passing LF | Q | 2 |
| 5 | Replace weight to LF | Q | 1 |
| 6 | RF forward passing LF | Q | 2 |
| 7 | LF forward passing RF | Q | 1 |
| 8 | RF forward | Q | 2 |
| | | | 4 bars |

## LADY

| Step | Description | Rhythm | Beat |
|------|-------------|--------|------|
| 1 | RF back | Q | 1 |
| 2 | LF back passing RF | Q | 2 |
| 3 | RF back passing LF | Q | 1 |
| 4 | LF back passing RF | Q | 2 |
| 5 | Replace weight to RF | Q | 1 |
| 6 | LF forward passing RF | Q | 2 |
| 7 | RF forward passing LF | Q | 1 |
| 8 | LF forward | Q | 2 |
| | | | 4 bars |

Separations can be repeated or linked as required and often precede turns.

# 5   PARALLEL WALKAROUND (LEFT & RIGHT)

Parallel Walkaround is usually danced from separations and is the simplest form of the many walkaround variations that exist in Merengue.

Start with the man's weight on RF (hip to right) and the lady's weight on LF (hip to left) feet slightly apart in close contact hold or double hold.

**Cuban Motion is used throughout.**

## MAN

| Step | Description | Rhythm | Beat |
|------|-------------|--------|------|
| 1-4 | Steps 1-4 of Separations (LF, RF, LF, RF) | Q's | 1,2,1,2 |
| 5-8 | Basic Movement turning L (LF, RF, LF, RF) to end in right side-by-side position facing opposite direction to lady retaining double hold | Q's | 1,2,1,2 |
| 9-12 | LF forward curving to R, continue with Progressive Basics Forward curving to R (RF, LF, RF) | Q's | 1,2,1,2 |
| 13-16 | Basic Movement turning R (LF, RF, LF, RF) to end in open facing position | Q's | 1,2,1,2 |
| 17-20 | Basic Movement turning R (LF, RF, LF, RF) to end in left side-by-side position facing opposite direction to lady retaining double hold | Q's | 1,2,1,2 |
| 21-24 | LF forward curving to L, continue with Progressive Basics Forward curving to L (RF, LF, RF) | Q's | 1,2,1,2 |
| 25-28 | Basic Movement turning L (LF, RF, LF, RF) to end in open facing position | Q's | 1,2,1,2 |
| 29-32 | Steps 5-8 of Separations (LF, RF, LF, RF) to end in close contact hold | Q's | 1,2,1,2 |

16 bars

# PARALLEL WALKAROUND (LEFT & RIGHT) (cont.)

## LADY

| Step | Description | Rhythm | Beat |
|------|-------------|--------|------|
| 1-4 | Steps 1-4 of Separations (RF, LF, RF, LF) | Q's | 1,2,1,2 |
| 5-8 | Basic Movement turning L (RF, LF, RF, LF) to end in right side-by-side position facing opposite direction to man retaining double hold | Q's | 1,2,1,2 |
| 9-12 | RF forward curving to R, continue with Progressive Basics Forward curving to R (LF, RF, LF) | Q's | 1,2,1,2 |
| 13-16 | Basic Movement turning R (RF, LF, RF, LF) to end in open facing position | Q's | 1,2,1,2 |
| 17-20 | Basic Movement turning R (RF, LF, RF, LF) to end in left side-by-side position facing opposite direction to man retaining double hold | Q's | 1,2,1,2 |
| 21-24 | RF forward curving to L, continue with Progressive Basics Forward curving to L (LF, RF, LF) | Q's | 1,2,1,2 |
| 25-28 | Basic Movement turning L (RF, LF, RF, LF) to end in open facing position | Q's | 1,2,1,2 |
| 29-32 | Steps 5-8 of Separations (RF, LF, RF, LF) to end in close contact hold | Q's | 1,2,1,2 |

16 bars

The Parallel Walkaround is often danced to left and right together in the simple way described above. This is a valuable way of learning to change direction during a step. However, the Parallel Walkaround can, of course, be danced to left or right separately and can be amalgamated into other moves. The curving action of the Walkaround is a cornerstone of many Merengue variations.

# 6  UNDERARM TURN RIGHT

Underarm Turn Right can be danced from close contact hold or open hold and is often amalgamated into other moves.

Start with the man's weight on RF (hip to right) and the lady's weight on LF (hip to left) feet slightly apart, in close contact hold. **Cuban Motion is used throughout.**

## MAN

| Step | Description | Rhythm | Beat |
|------|-------------|--------|------|
| 1-8 | Basic Movement (LF, RF etc), raise left arm on step 8 releasing hold with right arm preparing to turn lady to R | Q's | 1,2,1,2<br>1,2,1,2 |
| 9 | Continue Basic Movement (LF), commence to lead lady to turn R under left arm | Q | 1 |
| 10-16 | Continue Basic Movement (RF,LF etc) and continue to lead lady to complete 1 full turn to R, retaking close contact hold by step 16 | Q's | 2,1,2<br>1,2,1,2 |
| | | | 8 bars |

## LADY

| Step | Description | Rhythm | Beat |
|------|-------------|--------|------|
| 1-8 | Basic Movement (RF, LF etc) | Q's | 1,2,1,2<br>1,2,1,2 |
| 9 | RF to side, toe turned out, commence turn to R | Q | 1 |
| 10-16 | LF forward, continue to turn to R (RF, LF, RF, LF, RF, LF) completing 1 turn by step 16 retaking close contact hold | Q's | 2,1,2<br>1,2,1,2 |
| | | | 8 bars |

For progressive learning this step is best learned initially from and to close contact hold whilst dancing the Basic Movement. When more advanced it can be danced in double time and is often linked with Underarm Turn Left keeping joined hands above the head to create Continuous Underarm Turns.

# 7 UNDERARM TURN LEFT

Underarm Turn Left can be danced from close contact hold or open hold and is often amalgamated into other moves.

Start with the man's weight on RF (hip to right) and the lady's weight on LF (hip to left) feet slightly apart, in close contact hold. **Cuban Motion is used throughout.**

## MAN

| Step | Description | Rhythm | Beat |
|------|-------------|--------|------|
| 1-8 | Basic Movement (LF, RF etc), raise left arm on step 8 releasing hold with right arm preparing to turn lady to L | Q's | 1,2,1,2 1,2,1,2 |
| 9 | Continue Basic Movement (LF), commence to lead lady to turn L under left arm by moving left arm rightwards | Q | 1 |
| 10-16 | Continue Basic Movement (RF,LF etc) and continue to lead lady to complete 1 full turn to L, retaking close contact hold by step 16 | Q's | 2,1,2 1,2,1,2 |
| | | | 8 bars |

## LADY

| Step | Description | Rhythm | Beat |
|------|-------------|--------|------|
| 1-8 | Basic Movement (RF, LF etc) preparing to turn L on step 8, left foot to side, toe turned out | Q's | 1,2,1,2 1,2,1,2 |
| 9 | RF forward, commence turn to L | Q | 1 |
| 10-16 | LF forward, continue to turn to L (RF, LF, RF, LF, RF, LF) completing turn by step 16 retaking close contact hold | Q's | 2,1,2 1,2,1,2 |
| | | | 8 bars |

As with Underarm Turn Right, it is best for progressive learning to learn this step initially from and to close contact hold whilst dancing the Basic Movement. When more advanced Underarm Turn Left can be danced in double time and linked with Underarm Turn Right.

# 8   ARMLOCK TURN AND WALKAROUND

Armlock Turn and Walkaround is a step where the lady's turn to the left is "checked off " by retained double hold created an "armlock".

Start with the man's weight on RF (hip to right) and the lady's weight on LF (hip to left) feet slightly apart, in close contact hold or double hold.

**Cuban Motion is used throughout.**

## MAN

| Step | Description | Rhythm | Beat |
|------|-------------|--------|------|
| 1-4 | Steps 1-4 of Separations (LF, RF, LF, RF) | Q's | 1,2,1,2 |
| 5-8 | Basic Movement in place (LF, RF, LF, RF) making ¼ turn to L. Raise left arm on step 5 retaining double hold and leading lady to turn R under left arm (lady's right arm). The arms are gradually lowered to waist level by step 8 with the lady's left arm now behind her back. Man and lady are now in right side-by-side position facing the opposite direction. | Q's | 1,2,1,2 |
| 9-12 | LF forward curving to R, continue with Progressive Basics Forward (RF, LF, RF) curving to R | Q's | 1,2,1,2 |
| 13-16 | Basic Movement turning (LF, RF, LF, RF) making ½ turn to R raising left arm on step 13 and leading lady to turn L to end in either open facing position or close contact hold by step 16 | Q's | 1,2,1,2 |

8 bars

## LADY

| Step | Description | Rhythm | Beat |
|------|-------------|--------|------|
| 1-4 | Steps 1-4 of Separations (RF, LF, RF, LF) | Q's | 1,2,1,2 |
| 5 | RF forward, toe turned out, commence to turn to R retaining double hold | Q | 1 |

# ARMLOCK TURN AND WALKAROUND (cont.)

| Step | Description | Rhythm | Beat |
|------|-------------|--------|------|
| 6-8 | Continue to turn to R (LF, RF, LF) under right arm making ¾ turn by step 8 (lady's left arm is now behind and across her back) | Q's | 2,1,2 |
| 9-12 | RF forward curving to R, continue with Progressive Basics Forward (LF, RF, LF) curving to R | Q's | 1,2,1,2 |
| 13-16 | Basic Movement turning (RF, LF, RF, LF) making ½ turn to L to end in either open facing position or close contact hold by step 16 | Q's | 1,2,1,2 |

8 bars

The Armlock is often amalgamated with other moves such as the Wrap and is sometimes danced without the Walkaround. The 8-bar phrase described above incorporating the Walkaround and returning to close contact hold, is for learning purposes.

**The Armlock:** *this is used extensively in both Merengue & Salsa to "lock off" the lady's turn and change direction.*

# 9  WRAP AND WALKAROUND

The Wrap, also known as the Basket, is a figure common to Merengue and Salsa. The Wrap and Walkaround in Merengue is often linked with other double hold turning moves.

Start with the man's weight on RF (hip to right) and the lady's weight on LF (hip to left) feet slightly apart, in close contact hold or double hold.

**Cuban Motion is used throughout.**

## MAN

| Step | Description | Rhythm | Beat |
|------|-------------|--------|------|
| 1-4 | Basic Movement (LF, RF, LF, RF) | Q's | 1,2,1,2 |
| 5-8 | Steps 1-4 of Separations (LF, RF, LF, RF) | Q's | 1,2,1,2 |
| 9 | LF forward curving to R retaining double hold commencing to lead lady to turn L under left arm | Q | 1 |
| 10 | RF forward curving to R continuing to lead lady to turn L under left arm ending with lady on man's right side with joined arms at waist level | Q | 2 |
| 11-12 | Progressive Basics forward (LF, RF) curving to R | Q's | 1,2 |
| 13-16 | Basic Movement (LF, RF, LF, RF) turning to R raising left arm on step 13 leading lady to turn R under left arm to end in either open facing position or close contact hold | Q's | 1,2,1,2 |
| | | | 8 bars |

## LADY

| Step | Description | Rhythm | Beat |
|------|-------------|--------|------|
| 1-4 | Basic Movement (RF, LF, RF, LF) | Q's | 1,2,1,2 |
| 5-8 | Steps 1-4 of Separations (RF, LF, RF, LF) | Q's | 1,2,1,2 |
| 9 | RF forward, commence turn to L | Q | 1 |

## WRAP AND WALKAROUND (cont.)

| Step | Description | Rhythm | Beat |
|------|-------------|--------|------|
| 10 | LF back ending on man's right side with joined arms at waist level having made ½ turn over steps 5-6 | Q | 2 |
| 11-12 | Progressive Basics backward curving to L (RF, LF) | Q's | 1,2,1,2 |
| 13 | RF forward toe turned out, commence turn to R | Q | 1 |
| 14 | LF to side, continue to turn R | Q | 2 |
| 15 | RF to side and slightly back, continue to turn R | Q | 1 |
| 16 | LF to side to end either in open facing position or close contact hold having made ½ turn | Q | 2 |

8 bars

The suggested amount of turn is for learning purposes. If the man curves steps 5 – 8 to R the lady will make less than half a turn. If steps 9 – 12 are tightly curved the lady's footwork will be akin to a Top (i.e. toe to heel, toe turned out).

The Wrap position is very common in Merengue and is often linked with the Arm-lock to create continually turning moves.

*The Wrap: shown here in right side-by-side position, the man's right arm should provide a "frame" for the lady.*

# 10   OPPOSITION WALKAROUND

Opposition Walkaround is where the lady circles the man. It is the first step where the man is required to turn left and release hold.
Start with the man's weight on RF (hip to right) and the lady's weight on LF (hip to left) feet slightly apart, in close contact hold or double hold. **Cuban Motion is used throughout.**

## MAN

| Step | Description | Rhythm | Beat |
|------|-------------|--------|------|
| 1-4 | Steps 1-4 of Separations (LF, RF, LF, RF) releasing lady's left hand on step 4 | Q's | 1,2,1,2 |
| 5-8 | Basic Movement (LF, RF, LF, RF) making ¼ turn to L placing lady's right hand on man's right side | Q's | 1,2,1,2 |
| 9-16 | Release lady's right hand and continue Basic Movement (LF, RF, LF, RF) turning to L to complete 1 turn by step 16 retaking close contact hold | Q's | 1,2,1,2  1,2,1,2 |
| | | | 8 bars |

## LADY

| Step | Description | Rhythm | Beat |
|------|-------------|--------|------|
| 1-4 | Steps 1-4 of Separations (RF, LF, RF, LF) releasing man's right hand on step 4 | Q's | 1,2,1,2 |
| 5-8 | RF forward curving to R, continue with Progressive Basics Forward (LF, RF, LF) curving to R and commencing to circle the man | Q's | 1,2,1,2 |
| 9-16 | Release man's left hand and continue Progressive Basics Forward circling the man retaining contact with right hand on man's body to complete 1 full circle by step 16 retaking close contact hold | Q's | 1,2,1,2  1,2,1,2 |
| | | | 8 bars |

The man may "roll in" to his own arm more tightly, with more turn being made.

## 11   NATURAL TOP

When the Basic Movement in close contact hold is turned very tightly to the right, the foot positions automatically change to those akin to a step known internationally as the Natural Top as the feet accommodate the tightness of the turn. The man's feet are usually placed in front in the Natural Top in Club style Latin but can be placed behind as in the Competition style.

Start with the man's weight on RF (hip to right) and the lady's weight on LF (hip to left) feet slightly apart, in close contact hold or double hold.

**Cuban Motion is used throughout.**

## MAN

| Step | Description | Rhythm | Beat |
|------|-------------|--------|------|
| 1-4 | Steps 1-4 of Basic Movement (LF, RF, LF, RF) | Q's | 1,2,1,2 |
| 5 | LF to side tightly turning to R | Q | 1 |
| 6 | RF crosses in front or behind LF, toe to heel, toe turned out, continue to turn R | Q | 2 |
| 7-12 | Repeat steps 5 & 6 three times completing up to 2 turns over steps 5-12 | Q's | 1,2 1,2,1,2 |
| 13-16 | Steps 1-4 of Basic Movement (LF, RF, LF, RF) | Q's | 1,2,1,2 |
| | | | 8 bars |

## LADY

| Step | Description | Rhythm | Beat |
|------|-------------|--------|------|
| 1-4 | Steps 1-4 of Basic Movement (RF, LF, RF, LF) | Q's | 1,2,1,2 |
| 5 | RF crosses in front LF, toe to heel, toe turned out, tightly turning to R | Q | 1 |
| 6 | LF to side, continue to turn R | Q | 2 |
| 7-12 | Repeat steps 5 & 6 three times completing up to 2 turns over steps 5-12 | Q's | 1,2 1,2,1,2 |
| 13-16 | Steps 1-4 of Basic Movement (RF, LF, RF, LF) | Q's | 1,2,1,2 |
| | | | 8 bars |

## NATURAL TOP (cont.)

The Natural Top can also be danced turning to the left and is then known as the Reverse Top.

All Top movements can be amalgamated as required. The heel of the right foot should not lower until the left foot has started to move and when crossing in front it is important that the ball of the central foot should remain on one spot whilst the continuous turn is made. Slight Cuban Motion will ensure that the legs are slightly flexed when feet are crossed and will slightly straighten when apart.

Social dancers who are familiar with the Top movements may be surprised to find this figure listed as "Advanced" in Merengue. Tops, however, are more difficult than they appear and to dance Top movements well a sound understanding of partnering is required.

It is vital that to achieve a smooth, continuous rotation the man and lady should remain "square" to each other with the lady slightly offset to the man's right side. If the dancers become either side to side or face to face the turning effect is diminished.

# 12   HAND CHANGE TURN

Hand Change Turn is also an alternately turning figure with the development of the man changing hands behind his back. This move can be danced from close contact hold or open hold and is often amalgamated into other figures.

Start with the man's weight on RF (hip to right) and the lady's weight on LF (hip to left) feet slightly apart, in close contact hold.

**Cuban Motion is used throughout.**

## MAN

| Step | Description | Rhythm | Beat |
|------|-------------|--------|------|
| 1-4 | Basic Movement (LF, RF, LF, RF), raise left arm on step 4 releasing hold with right arm preparing to turn lady to R | Q's | 1,2,1,2 |
| 5-8 | Continue Basic Movement (LF, RF, LF, RF), leading lady to complete 1 full turn to R under left arm | Q's | 1,2,1,2 |
| 9 | LF forward, toe turned out, commence to turn L, lowering left arm to waist level | Q | 1 |
| 10 | RF forward, continuing to turn L, transferring lady's right hand into right hand | Q | 2 |
| 11 | LF forward, continuing to turn L, transferring lady's right hand into left hand behind back | Q | 1 |
| 12 | RF forward completing 1 full turn over steps 9-12 | Q | 2 |
| 13-16 | Basic Movement (LF, RF, LF, RF), leading lady to complete 1 full turn to L under left arm by moving left arm rightwards, retaking close contact hold on step 16 | Q's | 1,2,1,2 |

8 bars

# HAND CHANGE TURN (cont.)

## LADY

| Step | Description | Rhythm | Beat |
|------|-------------|--------|------|
| 1-4 | Basic Movement (RF, LF, R F, LF) preparing to turn R on step 4 | Q's | 1,2,1,2 |
| 5-8 | RF forward, toe turned out, continue turn to R (LF, RF, LF) under man's raised left arm completing 1 full turn by step 8 | Q's | 1,2,1,2 |
| 9-12 | Basic Movement (RF, LF, RF, LF) | Q's | 1,2,1,2 |
| 13-16 | RF forward, turn to L (LF, RF, LF) under man's raised left arm completing 1 full turn and retaking close contact hold on step 16 | Q's | 1,2,1,2 |
| | | | 8 bars |

An accurate placement of the lady's hand is essential when leading this step.

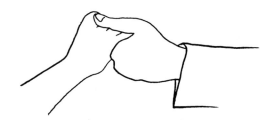

***Regular hand hold****: the man should be very "invitational" when offering his hand; note also how the lady's wrist is slightly dropped to receive leads through the arm to the "centre".*

## 13   MERENGUE CIRCLE

The Circle is an advanced variation where the lady is lead into right and left side-by-side positions in which a "Merengue Circle" is danced. This step can be danced from close contact hold or open hold and is often amalgamated into other figures.

Start with the man's weight on RF (hip to right) and the lady's weight on LF (hip to left) feet slightly apart, in close contact hold. **Cuban Motion is used throughout.**

## MAN

| Step | Description | Rhythm | Beat |
|------|-------------|--------|------|
| 1-4 | Basic Movement (LF, RF, LF, RF), raise left arm on step 4 releasing hold with right arm preparing to turn lady to R | Q's | 1,2,1,2 |
| 5-6 | Continue Basic Movement (LF, RF), leading lady to make 1 full turn R under left arm | Q's | 1,2 |
| 7-8 | Continue Basic Movement (LF, RF) turning tightly to L making ½ turn and place lady's right hand on right shoulder ending in left side-by-side position | Q's | 1,2 |
| 9-10 | Basic Movement progressing backward (LF, RF) and curving to R placing left arm around lady's waist in left side-by-side position | Q's | 1,2 |
| 11-12 | Continue Basic Movement progressing backward (LF, RF) curving to R passing lady to right side placing right arm around lady's waist in right side-by-side position | Q's | 1,2 |
| 13-16 | Basic Movement progressing forward (LF, RF, LF, RF) curving to R in right side-by-side position facing lady and retaking close contact hold by step 16 | Q's | 1,2,1,2 |

8 bars

# MERENGUE CIRCLE (cont.)

## LADY

| Step | Description | Rhythm | Beat |
|------|-------------|--------|------|
| 1-4 | Basic Movement (RF, LF, RF, LF) | Q's | 1,2,1,2 |
| 5-8 | Continue Basic Movement (RF, LF, RF, LF) turning tightly to R completing 1 turn by step 8 ending in left side-by-side position | Q's | 1,2,1,2 |
| 9-10 | Progressive Basics forward curving to R (RF, LF) (man will place his left arm around waist) | Q's | 1,2 |
| 11-12 | Continue Basic Movement progressing forward (RF, LF) passing to man's right side to right side-by-side position (man will place his right arm around waist) | Q's | 1,2 |
| 13-16 | Basic Movement progressing backward (RF, LF, RF, LF) curving to R in right side-by-side position facing man and retaking close contact hold by step 15 | Q's | 1,2,1,2 |
| | | | 8 bars |

It is important for both man and lady that, when dancing backwards, they do not pitch their weight backwards. Instead, they should place the stepping foot so as to create a base on which to transfer their weight.

## 14 ARM BREAKER

Arm Breaker is an underarm turning movement with an "unwinding" effect. Start with the man's weight on RF (hip to right) and the lady's weight on LF (hip to left) feet slightly apart, in close contact hold or double hold. **Cuban Motion is used throughout.**

### MAN

| Step | Description | Rhythm | Beat |
|------|-------------|--------|------|
| 1-4 | Steps 1-4 of Separations (LF, RF, LF, RF) | Q's | 1,2,1,2 |
| 5 | LF forward releasing lady's left hand placing lady's right hand behind and across her lower back and commencing to turn lady R | Q | 1 |
| 6 | RF forward transferring lady's right hand to man's right hand continuing to turn lady R | Q | 2 |
| 7-12 | LF to side and continue Basic Movement (RF, LF, RF, LF, RF). Raise right arm leading lady to make 1½ turns to R under right arm | Q'S | 1,2 1,2,1,2 |
| 13-16 | Continue Basic Movement (LF, RF, LF, RF) retaking close contact hold by step 16 | q'S | 1,2,1,2 |
| | | | 8 bars |

### LADY

| Step | Description | Rhythm | Beat |
|------|-------------|--------|------|
| 1-4 | Steps 1-4 of Separations (RF, LF, RF, LF) | Q's | 1,2,1,2 |
| 5 | RF forward toe turned out, release man's right hand and commencing to turn R taking right arm behind and across lower back | Q | 1 |
| 6 | LF forward continuing to turn R taking man's right hand completing ½ turn over steps 5-6 | Q | 2 |
| 7-12 | Continue to turn R (RF, LF, RF, LF, RF, LF) complete 1½ turns under man's right arm | Q's | 1,2 1,2,1,2 |
| 13-16 | Continue Basic Movement (RF, LF, RF, LF) retaking close contact hold by step 16 | Q's | 1,2,1,2 |
| | | | 8 bars |

An accurate placement of the lady's arm is essential when leading this step.

## 15   ROLLING OFF THE ARM

Rolling Off the Arm is an example of a step that is an advanced development from the wrap position.

Start with the man's weight on RF (hip to right) and the lady's weight on LF (hip to left) feet slightly apart, in close contact hold or double hold.

**Cuban Motion is used throughout.**

## MAN

| Step | Description | Rhythm | Beat |
|------|-------------|--------|------|
| 1-4 | Steps 1-4 of Separations (LF, RF, LF, RF) | Q's | 1,2,1,2 |
| 5-8 | LF forward curving to R, continue Progressive Basics forward (RF, LF, RF) retaining double hold raising left arm on step 5 leading lady to turn L under left arm ending with lady on man's right side with joined arms at waist level | Q's | 1,2,1,2 |
| 9 | LF forward curving to R releasing lady's right hand and commencing to lead lady to turn R | Q | 1 |
| 10 | RF forward, continue to curve to R, continuing to lead lady to turn R | Q | 2 |
| 11 | LF to side, cucaracha action, replace weight | Q | 1 |
| 12 | Replace weight to RF toe turned out commencing to turn R and leading lady to turn L releasing hold | Q | 2 |
| 13-16 | LF to side completing ¼ turn and continue Basic Movement (RF, LF, RF) retaking close contact hold by step 16 | Q | 1,2,1,2 |

8 bars

# ROLLING OFF THE ARM (cont.)

## LADY

| Step | Description | Rhythm | Beat |
|------|-------------|--------|------|
| 1-4 | Steps 1-4 of Separations (RF, LF, RF, LF) | Q's | 1,2,1,2 |
| 5 | RF forward | Q | 1 |
| 6 | LF forward toe turned out, commence turn to L | Q | 2 |
| 7 | RF to side and slightly back continuing to turn L | Q | 1 |
| 8 | LF back ending on man's right side with joined arms at waist level having made ½ turn | Q | 2 |
| 9 | RF to side toe turned out turning R | Q | 1 |
| 10 | LF forward continuing to turn R | Q | 2 |
| 11 | RF to side, cucaracha action, completing 1 full turn over steps 9-11 | Q | 1 |
| 12 | Replace weight to LF toe turned out commencing to turn L | Q | 2 |
| 13 | RF forward turning L | Q | 1 |
| 14 | LF forward toe turned out turning L | Q | 2 |
| 15 | RF forward turning L | Q | 1 |
| 16 | LF to side completing 1¼ turn over steps 12-16 retaking close contact hold | Q | 2 |

8 bars

Rolling off the Arm is a more flamboyant variation for dancers who have acquired a sound understanding of leading and following. On step 11 it is important that the lady's left wrist is dropped and her hand is placed firmly in the man's hand so that the dynamic is retained on the Cucaracha action.

In fast Merengues care will need to be taken when the man "collects" the lady at the end of the step as her last 1¼ turns will almost become a spin.

# SALSA

**Time signature:** 4/4 time. **Tempo:** 40 - 52 bpm. **FW:** ball flat throughout.

The music to which Salsa is danced covers many Cuban rhythms and is now beginning to encompass other Afro-Caribbean forms. Salsa the dance is relatively new in the UK but contains many elements of traditional Cuban social dance. It joins the list of Latin cultural dance forms that have grown out of developing traditional music.

Latin clubs for dancing increased their popularity in London during the 1970s. They were, however, largely divided into two categories: those which played Cuban music and those which played Colombian music – where Cumbia was danced. Salsa the dance as we now know it had not yet evolved in the UK. The visits of Salsa musical artists such as Tito Puente and Celia Cruz to London during this period played a large part in the evolution of the dance.

As the 1980s progressed, along came Lambada and several clubs started playing synthesized Brazilian music. The Lambada craze was hugely successful and brought many new people into Latin clubs. The dance seemed to incorporate Cumbia, Mambo and Samba and was danced in a tight rotational manner in close contact.

During the years following the Lambada craze Latin clubs returned to playing Salsa, even though many were not quite clear what to dance! Was it Lambada, was it Cumbia, was it Mambo? What has evolved is a fusion of them all.

Salsa the dance is generally danced as a three-beat step pattern in a four-beat bar, comprising a tap and three steps. The step pattern is initiated with the tap but there is still some inconsistency from club to club on which beat the tap occurs. However, as most social dancers will gravitate to the first beat, it is most common to see the tap actually danced on beat four. It is for this reason that the steps in this book place the tap at the end of the bar, i.e. 'and quick, quick, slow (rhythmic count)'. **Cuban Motion is used throughout** and there is also a slight, soft "lilting" action.

# SALSA

## LEVEL 1 - BEGINNER

| | |
|---|---|
| 1 | **The Basic Movement** |
| 2 | **Cucarachas** |
| 3 | **Open Break** |
| 4 | **Mambo Break** |
| 5 | **Opening Outs** |

## LEVEL 2 - INTERMEDIATE

| | |
|---|---|
| 6 | **Double Opening Outs** |
| 7 | **Underarm Turn Right** |
| 8 | **Underarm Turn Left** |
| 9 | **Double Hold Wrap** |
| 10 | **Salsa Turns** |

## LEVEL 3 - ADVANCED

| | |
|---|---|
| 11 | **The Chair** |
| 12 | **Armlock Turn to Left** |
| 13 | **Armlock Turn to Right** |
| 14 | **Hand Change Turn** |
| 15 | **Salsa Circle** |

# 1   THE BASIC MOVEMENT

The Basic Movement is usually danced in close contact hold and can be danced sideways to left or right, with strong turn to left or right. It can also be danced apart.

Start with the man's weight on RF (hip to right) and the lady's weight on LF (hip to left) feet slightly apart, in close contact hold. **Cuban Motion is used throughout.**

## MAN

| Step | Description | Rhythm | Beat |
|------|-------------|--------|------|
| 1 | LF to side | Q | 1 |
| 2 | RF closes towards LF | Q | 2 |
| 3-4 | LF to side, transfer weight (hip) to L and tap inside edge of ball of RF without weight | S | 3,4 |
| 5 | RF to side | Q | 1 |
| 6 | LF closes towards RF | Q | 2 |
| 7-8 | RF to side, transfer weight (hip) to R and tap inside edge of ball of LF without weight | S | 3,4 |
| | | | 2 bars |

## LADY

| Step | Description | Rhythm | Beat |
|------|-------------|--------|------|
| 1 | RF to side | Q | 1 |
| 2 | LF closes towards RF | Q | 2 |
| 3-4 | RF to side, transfer weight (hip) to R and tap inside edge of ball of LF without weight | S | 3,4 |
| 5 | LF to side | Q | 1 |
| 6 | RF closes towards LF | Q | 2 |
| 7-8 | LF to side, transfer weight (hip) to L and tap inside edge of ball of RF without weight | S | 3,4 |
| | | | 2 bars |

**The step pattern is initiated by a preparatory tap on beat four.** The lady should be slightly offset to the man's right in close contact hold. The Basic can be developed by stepping across and in front on steps 2 and 6 (Crossover Runs).

## 2   CUCARACHAS

Cucaracha is the Spanish word for cockroach. Cucarachas as a step are also known as Second Position Breaks. In Salsa, they are usually danced in close contact or open hold.

Start with the man's weight on RF (hip to right) and the lady's weight on LF (hip to left) feet slightly apart, in close contact hold. **Cuban Motion is used throughout. Prepare with a tap on beat four.**

## MAN

| Step | Description | Rhythm | Beat |
|------|-------------|--------|------|
| 1-8 | Basic Movement | Q,Q,S | 1,2,3,4 |
|  |  | Q,Q,S | 1,2,3,4 |
| 9 | LF to side on inside edge of ball of foot, transfer part weight keeping heel of RF on the floor | Q | 1 |
| 10 | Replace weight to RF | Q | 2 |
| 11-12 | Close LF to RF, transfer weight to LF and tap inside edge of ball of LF without weight | S | 3,4 |
| 13 | RF to side with part weight keeping heel of LF on the floor | Q | 1 |
| 14 | Replace weight to LF | Q | 2 |
| 15-16 | Close RF to LF, transfer weight to RF and tap inside edge of ball of LF without weight | S | 3,4 |

4 bars

## CUCARACHAS (cont.)

### LADY

| Step | Description | Rhythm | Beat |
|------|-------------|--------|------|
| 1-8 | Basic Movement | Q,Q,S | 1,2,3,4 |
|     |             | Q,Q,S | 1,2,3,4 |
| 9 | RF to side on inside edge of ball of foot, transfer part weight keeping heel of LF on the floor | Q | 1 |
| 10 | Replace weight to LF | Q | 2 |
| 11-12 | Close RF to LF, transfer weight to RF and tap inside edge of ball of LF without weight | S | 3,4 |
| 13 | LF to side with part weight keeping heel of RF on the floor | Q | 1 |
| 14 | Replace weight to RF | Q | 2 |
| 15-16 | Close LF to RF, transfer weight to LF and tap inside edge of ball of RF without weight | S | 3,4 |
|  |  |  | 4 bars |

**Cucarachas** are an important action in the learning process of Salsa as they are incorporated into many advanced moves. Note that on the slow count the hip does not transfer until beat four.

---

**THE BASIC MOVEMENT AND CUCARACHAS ARE USEFUL IN ESTABLISHING THE TIMING AND RHYTHMIC FEEL OF SALSA.**

---

# 3   OPEN BREAK

Open Break is sometimes taught as the first step in Salsa and although the man and lady step away from each other the step simply amounts to an "opening out" of the hip and is the first "opening out" type movement to learn in Salsa. This step is usually danced from close contact or open hold.

Start with the man's weight on RF (hip to right) and the lady's weight on LF (hip to left) feet slightly apart, in close contact hold.

**Cuban Motion is used throughout. Prepare with a tap on beat four.**

## MAN

| Step | Description | Rhythm | Beat |
|------|-------------|--------|------|
| 1-8 | Basic Movement | Q,Q,S | 1,2,3,4 |
|  |  | Q,Q,S | 1,2,3,4 |
| 9 | LF back, toe turned out, slight opening out position | Q | 1 |
| 10 | Replace weight to RF | Q | 2 |
| 11-12 | Close LF to RF, transfer weight to LF and tap inside edge of ball of RF without weight | S | 3,4 |
| 13 | RF back, toe turned out, slight opening out position | Q | 1 |
| 14 | Replace weight to LF | Q | 2 |
| 15-16 | Close RF to LF, transfer weight to RF and tap inside edge of ball of LF without weight | S | 3,4 |
|  |  |  | 4 bars |

## LADY

| Step | Description | Rhythm | Beat |
|------|-------------|--------|------|
| 1-8 | Basic Movement | Q,Q,S | 1,2,3,4 |
|  |  | Q,Q,S | 1,2,3,4 |
| 9 | RF back, toe turned out, slight opening out position | Q | 1 |
| 10 | Replace weight to LF | Q | 2 |

## OPEN BREAK (cont.)

| Step | Description | Rhythm | Beat |
|------|-------------|--------|------|
| 11-12 | Close RF to LF, transfer weight to RF and tap inside edge of ball of LF without weight | S | 3,4 |
| 13 | LF back, toe turned out, slight opening out position | Q | 1 |
| 14 | Replace weight to RF | Q | 2 |
| 15-16 | Close LF to RF, transfer weight to LF and tap inside edge of ball of RF without weight | S | 3,4 |
|  |  |  | 4 bars |

The Open Break is an important action in the learning process of Salsa as this step is the vehicle by which the technique of stepping backwards with part weight using a "catapult" action of the hip into an "opening out" type movement is learned.

When Open Breaks are danced from close contact hold the amount of opening out to left and right will be slight. When danced in open hold, up to one-eighth of a turn to left and right can be made.

***Open Break in Double Open hold:*** *Open Break can be danced in Close Hold or in Open Hold and is the Precede to many moves.*

# 4 MAMBO BREAK

Mambo Break is a forwards and backwards movement usually danced in close contact hold. It is the basic step of the American style Mambo.

Start with the man's weight on RF (hip to right) and the lady's weight on LF (hip to left) feet slightly apart, in close contact hold. **Cuban Motion is used throughout. Prepare with a tap on beat four.**

## MAN

| Step | Description | Rhythm | Beat |
|------|-------------|--------|------|
| 1 | LF forward | Q | 1 |
| 2 | Replace weight to RF | Q | 2 |
| 3-4 | Close LF to RF, transfer weight to LF and tap inside edge of ball of RF without weight | S | 3,4 |
| 5 | RF back | Q | 1 |
| 6 | Replace weight to LF | Q | 2 |
| 7-8 | Close RF to LF, transfer weight to RF and tap inside edge of ball of LF without weight | S | 3,4 |
|  |  |  | 2 bars |

## LADY

| Step | Description | Rhythm | Beat |
|------|-------------|--------|------|
| 1 | RF backward | Q | 1 |
| 2 | Replace weight to LF | Q | 2 |
| 3-4 | Close RF to LF, transfer weight to RF and tap inside edge of ball of LF without weight | S | 3,4 |
| 5 | LF forward | Q | 1 |
| 6 | Replace weight to RF | Q | 2 |
| 7-8 | Close LF to RF, transfer weight to LF and tap inside edge of ball of RF without weight | S | 3-4 |
|  |  |  | 2 bars |

When double hold is used, Step 1 can be danced taking the lady's hands above her head and behind her neck. When more advanced, Step 5 can be embellished with a "sinking" movement into the man's right leg and the lady's left leg.

# 5   OPENING OUTS

The Opening Outs consist of a Cucaracha action for the man whilst the lady dances an "Opening Out" type movement. This step is danced from close contact hold.

Start with the man's weight on RF (hip to right) and the lady's weight on LF (hip to left) feet slightly apart, in close contact hold.

**Cuban Motion is used throughout. Prepare with a tap on beat four.**

## MAN

| Step | Description | Rhythm | Beat |
|------|-------------|--------|------|
| 1-8 | Basic Movement | Q,Q,S | 1,2,3,4 |
|      |                | Q,Q,S | 1,2,3,4 |
| 9 | LF to side, Cucaracha action, leading lady to turn to R into opening out position taking left arm down and across body | Q | 1 |
| 10 | Replace weight to RF | Q | 2 |
| 11-12 | Close LF to RF, transfer weight to LF and tap inside edge of ball of RF without weight | S | 3,4 |
| 13 | RF to side, Cucaracha action, leading lady to turn to L into opening out position | Q | 1 |
| 14 | Replace weigh to LF | Q | 2 |
| 15-16 | Close RF to LF, transfer weight to RF and tap inside edge of ball of LF without weight | S | 3,4 |
|  |  |  | 4 bars |

## LADY

| Step | Description | Rhythm | Beat |
|------|-------------|--------|------|
| 1-8 | Basic Movement | Q,Q,S | 1,2,3,4 |
|      |                | Q,Q,S | 1,2,3,4 |
| 9 | RF back in opening out position making up to $\frac{1}{8}$ turn to R | Q | 1 |
| 10 | Replace weight to LF, commence to turn L | Q | 2 |

## OPENING OUTS (cont.)

| Step | Description | Rhythm | Beat |
|------|-------------|--------|------|
| 11-12 | RF to side, transfer weight to RF and tap inside edge of ball of LF without weight facing man | S | 3,4 |
| 13 | LF back in opening out position making up to $1/8$ turn to L | Q | 1 |
| 14 | Replace weight to RF, commence to turn R | Q | 2 |
| 15-16 | LF to side, transfer weight to LF and tap inside edge of ball of RF without weight facing man | S | 3,4 |
|  |  |  | 4 bars |

When danced from close contact hold the amount of turn for the lady is relatively slight.

It is useful to learn the first five steps of Salsa in hold. However, in a more advanced form of this step the man will release hold with his left hand passing the lady from side to side in order to widen the step. The lady will make up to half a turn when dancing this development, known as Advanced Opening Outs.

***Opening Out**: the man's right arm should "support" the lady when dancing Opening Outs on his right side, as shown here.*

## 6   DOUBLE OPENING OUTS

Double Opening Outs is also known in the USA as Fifth Position Breaks and is usually danced from close contact or double hold.

Start with the man's weight on RF (hip to right) and the lady's weight on LF (hip to left) feet slightly apart, in close contact hold.

**Cuban Motion is used throughout. Prepare with a tap on beat four.**

## MAN

| Step | Description | Rhythm | Beat |
|------|-------------|--------|------|
| 1-8 | Basic Movement | Q,Q,S | 1,2,3,4 |
| | | Q,Q,S | 1,2,3,4 |
| 9 | LF back in opening out position making up to ¼ turn to L | Q | 1 |
| 10 | Replace weight to RF in PP | Q | 2 |
| 11-12 | LF to side, transfer weight to LF and tap inside edge of ball of RF without weight turning back to face lady passing through close hold | S | 3,4 |
| 13 | RF back in opening out position making up to ⅝ turn to R releasing hold with right hand only | Q | 1 |
| 14 | Replace weight to LF in left side-by-side position | Q | 2 |
| 15-16 | RF to side, transfer weight to RF and tap inside edge of ball of LF without weight turning back to face lady passing through close hold | S | 3,4 |
| 17-24 | Repeat steps 9-16 | Q,Q,S | 1,2,3,4 |
| | | Q,Q,S | 1,2,3,4 |
| 25-32 | Basic Movement gradually returning to close contact hold | Q,Q,S | 1,2,3,4 |
| | | Q,Q,S | 1,2,3,4 |
| | | | 8 bars |

# DOUBLE OPENING OUTS (cont.)

## LADY

| Step | Description | Rhythm | Beat |
|------|-------------|--------|------|
| 1-8 | Basic Movement | Q,Q,S | 1,2,3,4 |
|  |  | Q,Q,S | 1,2,3,4 |
| 9 | RF back in opening out position making up to ¼ turn to R | Q | 1 |
| 10 | Replace weight to LF in PP | Q | 2 |
| 11-12 | RF to side, transfer weight to RF and tap inside edge of ball of LF without weight turning back to face man passing through close hold | S | 3,4 |
| 13 | LF back in opening out position making up to $^5/_8$ turn to L releasing hold with left hand only | Q | 1 |
| 14 | Replace weight to RF in left side-by-side position | Q | 2 |
| 15-16 | LF to side, transfer weight to LF and tap inside edge of ball of RF without weight turning back to face man passing through close hold | S | 3,4 |
| 17-24 | Repeat steps 9-16 | Q,Q,S | 1,2,3,4 |
|  |  | Q,Q,S | 1,2,3,4 |
| 25-32 | Basic Movement gradually returning to close contact hold | Q,Q,S | 1,2,3,4 |
|  |  | Q,Q,S | 1,2,3,4 |
|  |  |  | 8 bars |

The Double Opening Outs is an important step in a progressive learning process as it is the first time that hold **must** be released and whereby the man is required to make more turn on his "opening out" movements.

The suggestion of releasing hold with one hand only and retaining hold with the man's left and the lady's right hands throughout the figure makes the step easier to learn. More advanced dancers in clubs may dance this step from right side-by-side position with the man's right arm around the lady's waist, to left side-by-side position with the man's left arm around the lady's waist and lady's right arm around the man's upper back. **See page 83 for a diagram.**

# 7 UNDERARM TURN RIGHT

Underarm Turn Right, also known as an Alemana Turn, is usually danced from close contact or open hold and is often danced in double hold with the joined hands above the head. It is amalgamated into many other moves.

Start with the man's weight on RF (hip to right) and the lady's weight on LF (hip to left) feet slightly apart, in close contact hold. **Cuban Motion is used throughout. Prepare with a tap on beat four.**

## MAN

| Step | Description | Rhythm | Beat |
|------|-------------|--------|------|
| 1-8 | Basic Movement, raise left arm on step 8 | Q,Q,S | 1,2,3,4 |
| | releasing hold with right arm preparing to turn lady to R | Q,Q,S | 1,2,3,4 |
| 9 | Continue Basic Movement, commence to lead lady to turn R under left arm | Q | 1 |
| 10-16 | Continue Basic Movement and continue to lead lady to complete 1 full turn to R, retaking close contact hold by step 16 | Q,S Q,Q,S | 2,3,4 1,2,3,4 |
| | | | 4 bars |

## LADY

| Step | Description | Rhythm | Beat |
|------|-------------|--------|------|
| 1-8 | Basic Movement | Q,Q,S Q,Q,S | 1,2,3,4 1,2,3,4 |
| 9 | RF to side, toe turned out, commence to turn R | Q | 1 |
| 10-16 | LF forward, continue Basic Movement turning tightly to R completing 1 turn by step 16 retaking close contact hold | Q,S Q,Q,S | 2,3,4 1,2,3,4 |
| | | | 4 bars |

Underarm Turn Right is used in an infinite variety of ways but for progressive learning is best learned initially from and to close hold whilst dancing the Basic Movement. When more advanced, the lady's turn can be completed in one bar.

# 8   UNDERARM TURN LEFT

Underarm Turn Left is usually danced from close contact or open hold and is often danced in double hold with the joined hands above the head. It is amalgamated into many other moves.

Start with the man's weight on RF (hip to right) and the lady's weight on LF (hip to left) feet slightly apart, in close contact hold. **Cuban Motion is used throughout. Prepare with a tap on beat four.**

## MAN

| Step | Description | Rhythm | Beat |
|------|-------------|--------|------|
| 1-8 | Basic Movement raise left arm on step 8 | Q,Q,S | 1,2,3,4 |
| | releasing hold with right arm preparing to turn lady to L | Q,Q,S | 1,2,3,4 |
| 9 | Continue Basic Movement, commence to lead lady to turn L under left arm by moving left arm rightwards | Q | 1 |
| 10-16 | Continue Basic Movement and continue to lead lady to turn to L completing turn by step 16 retaking close contact hold | Q,S <br> Q,Q,S | 2,3,4 <br> 1,2,3,4 |
| | | | 4 bars |

## LADY

| Step | Description | Rhythm | Beat |
|------|-------------|--------|------|
| 1-8 | Basic Movement | Q,Q,S <br> Q,Q,S | 1,2,3,4 <br> 1,2,3,4 |
| 9 | RF forward, commence turn to L | Q | 1 |
| 10-16 | LF forward, continue Basic Movement turning tightly to L completing 1 turn by step 16 retaking close contact hold | Q,S <br> Q,Q,S | 2,3,4 <br> 1,2,3,4 |
| | | | 4 bars |

When more advanced the lady's turn can be completed in one bar. Advanced combinations of Underarm Turns to Right and Left are often danced retaining double hold with the joined hands above the head and improvisation is common with underarm turns.

# 9   DOUBLE HOLD WRAP

The Double Hold Wrap, also known as Half Turns and the Basket, is a popular club style move where the man brings the lady into his right side.

Start with the man's weight on RF (hip to right) and the lady's weight on LF (hip to left) feet slightly apart, in close contact hold.

**Cuban Motion is used throughout. Prepare with a tap on beat four.**

## MAN

| Step | Description | Rhythm | Beat |
|------|-------------|--------|------|
| 1-8 | Basic Movement changing to double hold | Q,Q,S | 1,2,3,4 |
| | by step 8 | Q,Q,S | 1,2,3,4 |
| 9-16 | Open Breaks in double hold | Q,Q,S | 1,2,3,4 |
| | | Q,Q,S | 1,2,3,4 |
| 17 | LF back in Open Break position | Q | 1 |
| 18 | Replace weight to RF, commence to turn lady to L | Q | 2 |
| 19-20 | LF forward, transfer weight to LF and tap inside edge of ball of RF without weight continuing to turn lady to L | S | 3,4 |
| 21 | RF forward, toe turned out checking off lady's turn into the crook of man's arm in double hold wrap position | Q | 1 |
| 22 | Replace weight to LF leading lady to commence to turn to R | Q | 2 |
| 23-24 | RF back, transfer weight to RF and tap inside edge of ball of LF without weight continuing to turn lady to R | S | 3,4 |
| 25-32 | Repeat steps 17-24 retaining double hold or preparing to retake close contact hold on step 32 | Q,Q,S | 1,2,3,4 |
| | | Q,Q,S | 1,2,3,4 |

8 bars

# DOUBLE HOLD WRAP (cont.)

## LADY

| Step | Description | Rhythm | Beat |
|------|-------------|--------|------|
| 1-8 | Basic Movement changing to double hold | Q,Q,S | 1,2,3,4 |
| | by step 8 | Q,Q,S | 1,2,3,4 |
| 9-16 | Open Breaks in double hold | Q,Q,S | 1,2,3,4 |
| | | Q,Q,S | 1,2,3,4 |
| 17 | RF back in Open Break position | Q | 1 |
| 18 | Replace weight to LF, commencing turn to L | Q | 2 |
| 19-20 | RF to side, transfer weight to RF and tap inside edge of ball of LF without weight continuing turn to L completing ½ turn ending in right side-by-side double hold wrap position | S | 3,4 |
| 21 | LF back | Q | 1 |
| 22 | RF forward, toe turned out, commencing turn to R | Q | 2 |
| 23-24 | LF to side, transfer weight to LF and tap inside edge of ball of RF without weight continuing turn to R completing ½ turn | S | 3,4 |
| 25-32 | Repeat steps 17-24 retaining double hold or preparing to retake close contact hold on step 32 | Q,Q,S Q,Q,S | 1,2,3,4 1,2,3,4 |
| | | | 8 bars |

The Double Hold Wrap is the most basic form of Wrap type movements. When more advanced the Wrap is often danced in right hand to right hand hold only, the most popular variations being the Neck and Waist wrap. The suggestion of initially dancing the step from Basic Movement and Open Breaks is for learning purposes.

The technique of the man turning out the leading foot as he checks off the lady's movement is to help keep the focus to the lady. Note that on the back steps for both man and lady some weight is retained on the inside edge of the front foot.

## 10   SALSA TURNS

Salsa Turns, also known as Changing Places, is an essential and popular move in Club-style Salsa. It is a movement whereby the man and lady continuously change places.

Start with the man's weight on RF (hip to right) and the lady's weight on LF (hip to left) feet slightly apart, in close contact hold.

**Cuban Motion is used throughout. Prepare with a tap on beat four.**

## MAN

| Step | Description | Rhythm | Beat |
|------|-------------|--------|------|
| 1-8 | Basic Movement changing to double hold | Q,Q,S | 1,2,3,4 |
| | by step 8 | Q,Q,S | 1,2,3,4 |
| 9-16 | Open Breaks in double hold | Q,Q,S | 1,2,3,4 |
| | | Q,Q,S | 1,2,3,4 |
| 17 | LF back in Open Break position | Q | 1 |
| 18 | Replace weight to RF, commence to turn R leading lady to turn L under left arm | Q | 2 |
| 19-20 | LF to side, continue to turn R, transfer weight to LF and tap inside edge of ball of RF without weight, continue to turn lady to L | S | 3,4 |
| 21 | RF back in Open Break position having made ½ turn over steps 18-21 | Q | 1 |
| 22 | Replace weight to LF, commence to turn L under lady's left arm | Q | 2 |
| 23-24 | RF to side, continue to turn L, transfer weight to RF and tap inside edge of ball of LF without weight | S | 3,4 |
| 25 | LF back in Open Break Position having made ½ turn over steps 22-25 | Q | 1 |
| 26 | Replace weight to RF | Q | 2 |
| 27-28 | LF forward, transfer weight to LF and tap inside edge of ball of RF without weight | S | 3,4 |
| 29-32 | Open Breaks in double hold retaking close contact hold by step 32 | Q,Q,S | 1,2,3,4 |

8 bars

## SALSA TURNS (cont.)

## LADY

| Step | Description | Rhythm | Beat |
|------|-------------|--------|------|
| 1-8 | Basic Movement changing to double hold | Q,Q,S | 1,2,3,4 |
| | by step 8 | Q,Q,S | 1,2,3,4 |
| 9-16 | Open Breaks in double hold | Q,Q,S | 1,2,3,4 |
| | | Q,Q,S | 1,2,3,4 |
| 17 | RF back in Open Break position | Q | 1 |
| 18 | Replace weight to LF, commence to turn L under man's left arm | Q | 2 |
| 19-20 | RF to side, continue to turn L, transfer weight to RF and tap inside edge of ball of LF without weight | S | 3,4 |
| 21 | LF back in Open Break position having made ½ turn over steps 18-21 | Q | 1 |
| 22 | Replace weight to RF, commence to turn R | Q | 2 |
| 23-24 | LF to side, continue to turn R, transfer weight to LF and tap inside edge of ball of RF without weight (man turning L under lady's left arm) | S | 3,4 |
| 25 | RF back in Open Break Position having made ½ turn over steps 22-25 | Q | 1 |
| 26 | Replace weight to LF | Q | 2 |
| 27-28 | RF forward, transfer weight to RF and tap inside edge of ball of LF without weight | S | 3,4 |
| 29-32 | Open Breaks in double hold retaking close contact hold by step 32 | Q,Q,S | 1,2,3,4 |
| | | | 8 bars |

The Salsa Turns require a sound understanding of leading and following as the step produces a great amount of impetus and speed. As more speed is produced in fast pieces of Salsa the weight is kept more forward onto the inside edge of the front foot on the back steps for both man and lady so that the Cuban Motion hip action acts as a "catapult" effect. The suggestion of dancing this step initially in double hold is for learning purposes. Double hold allows the man to "shape" to the right when turning right and to the left when turning left. This will assist in leading the step.

## 11   THE CHAIR

The Chair, which is a development of the Wrap, is a very popular move in Club Salsa where the lady dances a "sitting" type movement on the man's right thigh.

Start with the man's weight on RF (hip to right) and the lady's weight on LF (hip to left) feet slightly apart, in close contact hold.

**Cuban Motion is used throughout. Prepare with a tap on beat four.**

## MAN

| Step | Description | Rhythm | Beat |
|------|-------------|--------|------|
| 1-8 | Basic Movement changing to double hold | Q,Q,S | 1,2,3,4 |
|  | by step 8 | Q,Q,S | 1,2,3,4 |
| 9-16 | Open Breaks in double hold | Q,Q,S | 1,2,3,4 |
|  |  | Q,Q,S | 1,2,3,4 |
| 17 | LF back, Open Break | Q | 1 |
| 18 | Replace weight to RF, commence to turn lady to L | Q | 2 |
| 19-20 | LF to side, wide step leading lady to turn L into Wrap position | S | 3,4 |
| 21-22 | Flex knees and lead lady to "sit" on right thigh | Q,Q | 1,2 |
| 23-24 | Replace weight to RF leading lady to turn to R | S | 3,4 |
| 25-32 | Repeat steps 17-24 retaining double hold or preparing to retake close contact hold on step 32 | Q,Q,S | 1,2,3,4 |
|  |  | Q,Q,S | 1,2,3,4 |

8 bars

## LADY

| Step | Description | Rhythm | Beat |
|------|-------------|--------|------|
| 1-8 | Basic Movement changing to double hold | Q,Q,S | 1,2,3,4 |
|  | by step 8 | Q,Q,S | 1,2,3,4 |
| 9-16 | Open Breaks in double hold | Q,Q,S | 1,2,3,4 |
|  |  | Q,Q,S | 1,2,3,4 |

# THE CHAIR (cont.)

| Step | Description | Rhythm | Beat |
|------|-------------|--------|------|
| 17 | RF back, Open Break | Q | 1 |
| 18 | Replace weight to LF, commencing turn to L | Q | 2 |
| 19-20 | RF to side, turn to L completing ½ turn ending in double hold wrap position | S | 3,4 |
| 21-22 | "Sit" on man's thigh, weight on RF | Q,Q | 1,2 |
| 23-24 | Turn to R completing ½ turn and transfer weight to LF | S | 3,4 |
| 25-32 | Repeat steps 17-24 preparing to retake close contact or double hold on step 32 | Q,Q,S  Q,Q,S | 1,2,3,4  1,2,3,4 |
| | | | 8 bars |

It is important that to lead The Chair **without force** the man must keep his hips tucked under on steps 19-22 and must not drive the lady downwards, rather "invite" her to sit on his thigh whilst in the wrap position.

When very advanced the man can lead the lady into a backbend movement over his right arm in place of the sitting movement.

**The Chair:** *the man's right arm should provide support for the lady and can assist the lead.*

## 12 ARMLOCK TURN TO LEFT

The Armlock Turn to Left is a step where the lady's turn to the left is "checked off" by retaining double hold creating an "armlock".

Start with the man's weight on RF (hip to right) and the lady's weight on LF (hip to left) feet slightly apart, in close contact hold.

**Cuban Motion is used throughout. Prepare with a tap on beat four.**

## MAN

| Step | Description | Rhythm | Beat |
|------|-------------|--------|------|
| 1-8 | Basic Movement changing to double hold | Q,Q,S | 1,2,3,4 |
| | by step 8 | Q,Q,S | 1,2,3,4 |
| 9-20 | Open Breaks in double hold | Q,Q,S | 1,2,3,4 |
| | | Q,Q,S | 1,2,3,4 |
| | | Q,Q,S | 1,2,3,4 |
| 21-24 | Basic Movement making up to ¼ turn to R. Raise right arm on step 21 retaining double hold and leading lady to turn L under right arm (lady's right arm). The arms are gradually lowered to waist level by step 24 with the lady's right arm now behind her back in Armlock. Man and lady are now in left side-by-side position facing the opposite direction. | Q,Q,S | 1,2,3,4 |
| 25-28 | LF back, Open Break, raising right arm on step 27 and leading lady to "unwind" to R. (Man makes up to ¼ turn to L over steps 26-28) | Q,Q,S | 1,2,3,4 |
| 29-32 | Basic Movement retaking close contact or double hold by step 32 | Q,Q,S | 1,2,3,4 |

8 bars

# ARMLOCK TURN TO LEFT (cont.)

## LADY

| Step | Description | Rhythm | Beat |
|------|-------------|--------|------|
| 1-8 | Basic Movement changing to double hold | Q,Q,S | 1,2,3,4 |
| | by step 8 | Q,Q,S | 1,2,3,4 |
| 9-20 | Open Breaks in double hold | Q,Q,S | 1,2,3,4 |
| | | Q,Q,S | 1,2,3,4 |
| | | Q,Q,S | 1,2,3,4 |
| 21-24 | Basic Movement turning tightly to L under | Q,Q,S | 1,2,3,4 |
| | man's right arm completing ¾ turn by step | | |
| | 24, retaining double hold (lady's right arm | | |
| | is now behind and across her back) | | |
| 25 | RF back, Open Break | Q | 1 |
| 26 | Replace weight to LF and commence to turn | Q | 2 |
| | tightly to R | | |
| 27-28 | RF forward, continue to turn tightly to R, | S | 3,4 |
| | transfer weight to RF and tap inside edge of | | |
| | ball of LF without weight, completing ¾ | | |
| | turn to R over steps 26-28 | | |
| 29-32 | Basic Movement retaking close contact or | Q,Q,S | 1,2,3,4 |
| | double hold by step 32 | | |

8 bars

It is important that the first turn to the left for the lady is not lead too early and the unwinding turn to the right is lead principally through the man's left and lady's right hands.

The suggestion of returning to Basic Movement is for learning purposes. The Armlock Turn to Left is, however, often linked with the Armlock Turn to Right to make a stylish rotational combination.

# 13  ARMLOCK TURN TO RIGHT

As in Merengue, the Armlock Turn is a step where the lady's turn to the right is "checked off" by retaining double hold creating an "armlock".

Start with the man's weight on RF (hip to right) and the lady's weight on LF (hip to left) feet slightly apart, in close contact hold.

**Cuban Motion is used throughout. Prepare with a tap on beat four.**

## MAN

| Step | Description | Rhythm | Beat |
|------|-------------|--------|------|
| 1-8 | Basic Movement changing to double hold | Q,Q,S | 1,2,3,4 |
|  | by step 8 | Q,Q,S | 1,2,3,4 |
| 9-20 | Open Breaks in double hold | Q,Q,S | 1,2,3,4 |
|  |  | Q,Q,S | 1,2,3,4 |
|  |  | Q,Q,S | 1,2,3,4 |
| 21-24 | Basic Movement making up to ¼ turn to L. Raise left arm on step 21 retaining double hold and leading lady to turn R under left arm (lady's right arm). The arms are gradually lowered to waist level by step 24 with the lady's left arm now behind her back in Armlock. Man and lady are now in right side-by-side position facing the opposite direction. | Q,Q,S | 1,2,3,4 |
| 25-28 | LF back, Open Break, raising left arm on step 27 and leading lady to "unwind" to L. (Man makes up to ¼ turn to R over steps 26-28) | Q,Q,S | 1,2,3,4 |
| 29-32 | Basic Movement leading lady to make 1 further turn to L, retaking close contact or double hold | Q,Q,S | 1,2,3,4 |

8 bars

## ARMLOCK TURN TO RIGHT (cont.)

## LADY

| Step | Description | Rhythm | Beat |
|------|-------------|--------|------|
| 1-8 | Basic Movement changing to double hold | Q,Q,S | 1,2,3,4 |
| | by step 8 | Q,Q,S | 1,2,3,4 |
| 9-20 | Open Breaks in double hold | Q,Q,S | 1,2,3,4 |
| | | Q,Q,S | 1,2,3,4 |
| | | Q,Q,S | 1,2,3,4 |
| 21-24 | LF forward, Basic Movement turning tightly to R under man's left arm completing ¾ turn by step 24, retaining double hold (lady's left arm is now behind and across her back) | Q,Q,S | 1,2,3,4 |
| 25 | RF back, Open Break | Q | 1 |
| 26 | Replace weight to LF and commence to turn tightly to L | Q | 2 |
| 27-28 | RF forward, continue to turn tightly to L, transfer weight to RF and tap inside edge of ball of LF without weight, completing ¾ turn to L over steps 26-28 | S | 3,4 |
| 29-32 | Basic Movement turning tightly to L making 1 further complete turn retaking close contact or double hold | Q,Q,S | 1,2,3,4 |
| | | | 8 bars |

It is important that the first turn to the right for the lady is not lead too early and the unwinding turn to the left is lead principally through the man's right and lady's left hands. This can, however, also be assisted by the man shaping his body to the right on the lady's left turn.

# 14   HAND CHANGE TURN

The Hand Change Turn is an alternately turning figure with the development of the man changing hands behind his back. This move can be danced from close contact hold or open hold and is often amalgamated into other figures.

Start with the man's weight on RF (hip to right) and the lady's weight on LF (hip to left) feet slightly apart, in close contact hold.

**Cuban Motion is used throughout. Prepare with a tap on beat four.**

## MAN

| Step | Description | Rhythm | Beat |
|------|-------------|--------|------|
| 1-4 | Basic Movement, raise left arm on step 4 releasing hold with right arm preparing to turn lady to L | Q,Q,S | 1,2,3,4 |
| 5-8 | Basic Movement, leading lady to turn L under left arm | Q,Q,S | 1,2,3,4 |
| 9 | LF forward, toe turned out, commence to turn L, lowering left arm to waist level | Q | 1 |
| 10 | RF forward, continuing to turn L, transferring lady's right hand into right hand | Q | 2 |
| 11 | LF forward, continuing to turn L, transferring lady's right hand into left hand behind back | Q | 3 |
| 12 | RF to side, tap inside edge of ball of RF without weight continuing to turn L | Q | 4 |
| 13-16 | Basic Movement, leading lady to turn L under left arm preparing to retake close contact hold | Q,Q,S | 1,2,3,4 |

4 bars

## LADY

| Step | Description | Rhythm | Beat |
|------|-------------|--------|------|
| 1-4 | Basic Movement | Q,Q,S | 1,2,3,4 |
| 5-8 | LF forward, toe turned out, continue Basic Movement turning tightly to L completing 1 turn by step 8 | Q,Q,S | 1,2,3,4 |

## HAND CHANGE TURN (cont.)

| Step | Description | Rhythm | Beat |
|------|-------------|--------|------|
| 9-12 | Basic Movement | Q,Q,S | 1,2,3,4 |
| 13-16 | LF forward, toe turned out, continue Basic Movement turning tightly to L completing 1 turn by step 16 preparing to retake close contact hold | Q,Q,S | 1,2,3,4 |
| | | | 4 bars |

It is important for the man to indicate very clearly that the Hand Change Turn is his intention so that the lady will dance the Basic Movement in place whilst he turns.

**Palm to palm hand hold:**
*the man may also
occasionally hold the
lady's wrist.*

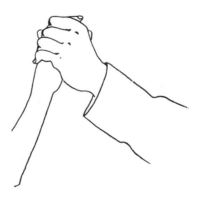

# 15   SALSA CIRCLE

The Circle is an advanced variation where the lady is lead into right and left side-by-side positions in which a "Salsa Circle" is danced.

Start with the man's weight on RF (hip to right) and the lady's weight on LF (hip to left) feet slightly apart, in close contact hold. **Cuban Motion is used throughout. Prepare with a tap on beat four.**

## MAN

| Step | Description | Rhythm | Beat |
|------|-------------|--------|------|
| 1-8 | Basic Movement, raise left arm on step 8 releasing hold with right arm preparing to turn lady to R | Q,Q,S Q,Q,S | 1,2,3,4 1,2,3,4 |
| 9-10 | Continue Basic Movement, leading lady to make 1 full turn R under left arm | Q,Q | 1,2 |
| 11-12 | Continue Basic Movement turning tightly to L making ½ turn and place lady's right hand on right shoulder ending in left side-by-side position | S | 3,4 |
| 13-16 | Basic Movement progressing backward and curving to R placing left arm around lady's waist in left side-by-side position by step 16 | Q,Q,S | 1,2,3,4 |
| 17-20 | Continue Basic Movement progressing backward curving to R in left side-by-side position | Q,Q,S | 1,2,3,4 |
| 21-24 | Continue Basic Movement progressing backward curving to R passing lady to right side placing right arm around lady's waist in right side-by-side position | Q,Q,S | 1,2,3,4 |
| 25-32 | Basic Movement progressing forward curving to R in right side-by-side position facing lady and retaking close contact hold by step 32 | Q,Q,S Q,Q,S | 1,2,3,4 1,2,3,4 |

8 bars

## SALSA CIRCLE (cont.)

### LADY

| Step | Description | Rhythm | Beat |
|------|-------------|--------|------|
| 1-8 | Basic Movement | Q,Q,S | 1,2,3,4 |
| | | Q,Q,S | 1,2,3,4 |
| 9-12 | Continue Basic Movement turning tightly to R completing 1 turn by step 12 ending in left side-by-side position | Q,Q,S | 1,2,3,4 |
| 13-20 | Basic Movement progressing forward and curving to R (man will place his left arm around waist) | Q,Q,S | 1,2,3,4 |
| | | Q,Q,S | 1,2,3,4 |
| 21-24 | Continue Basic Movement progressing forward curving to R passing to man's right side to right side-by-side position (man will place his right arm around waist) | Q,Q,S | 1,2,3,4 |
| 25-32 | Basic Movement progressing backward curving to R in right side-by-side position facing man and retaking close contact hold by step 32 | Q,Q,S | 1,2,3,4 |
| | | Q,Q,S | 1,2,3,4 |
| | | | 8 bars |

Advanced dancers in Salsa may eliminate the tap or replace it with a flick. This is particularly effective in the "circling" steps of this figure.

---

**ALTHOUGH THE SALSA STEPS IN THIS BOOK PLACE THE TAP ON BEAT 4, MORE ADVANCED DANCERS CAN TAP ON 1, PLACING THE BREAK STEP ON THE "OFF BEAT".**

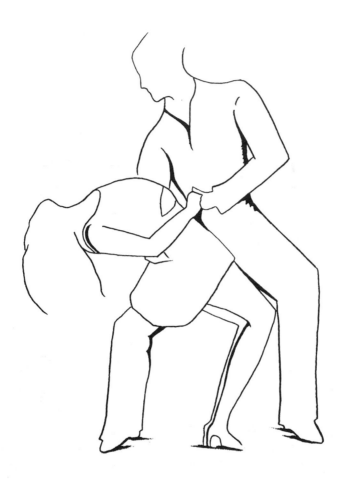

"REMEMBER THAT STEPS ARE ONLY SECONDARY,
IT IS YOUR BALANCE THAT IS OF
PRIMARY IMPORTANCE"

- VICTOR SILVESTER, 1930

# AN INTRODUCTION TO
# OTHER LATIN RHYTHMS

In this section, you are provided with five basic steps in each of two more dances covered by the umbrella of *Salsa:* Mambo and Cha Cha Cha

# MAMBO

**Time signature:** 4/4 time. **Tempo:** 36 - 52 bpm. **FW:** ball flat throughout.

Mambo is an Afro-Cuban musical form evolving from the Congalese religious cults. However, the big band Mambo was developed in the USA and largely in New York. A "Mambo Section" in Salsa is a musical phrase of contrasting riffs for front line instruments, e.g. setting trumpets against saxophones or trombones.

Mambo as a couple dance has been popular and standardised in America since its heyday of the 1950s when the Palladium Dance Hall in New York had an all Mambo policy featuring the big bands of Tito Puente, Tito Rodriguez and Machito, whilst on the West Coast, Perez Prado developed his own particular Mambo sound.

The continuing popularity of the Mambo has been helped by the dance being featured in movies such as The Mambo Kings and Dirty Dancing. The couple dance described in this book is based upon the American style Mambo featured in these films and should not be confused with the authentic Cuban folkloric Mambo. More and more dance studios today are offering tuition in Mambo and it would appear that there is a growing awareness that not all pieces of Salsa (music) are Mambos, and vice versa. Therefore, there is a growing acceptance that Mambo the dance and Salsa the dance are not the same.

Mambo today is also danced in a more sensual manner than its 1950's predecessor and has been chosen as the third dance in this book because its official "off beat" timing makes it more difficult than Merengue and Salsa for social dancers and, indeed, it is very common to see people dancing the "break" step on the first beat of the bar rather than on beat two, which is generally accepted as being correct. The basic figures in this book are Mambo steps that will introduce the Salsero to a long-standing and exciting dance.

The American club style Mambo is a spot dance and an in-depth understanding of Cuban Motion is required. It is usually danced in close hold.

# MAMBO

ALTHOUGH THESE FIRST FIVE BASIC MAMBO STEPS ARE SHOWN WITH THE "BREAK" STEP ON COUNT 2, IN CLUBS IT IS OFTEN DANCED ON COUNT 1.

# 1   THE BASIC MOVEMENT

The Mambo is standardised on the "off beat", i.e. the break step is on the count of 2. It is usually danced in close hold (slightly apart), but can be danced in open hold or apart. Start with the man's weight on RF (hip to right) and the lady's weight on LF (hip to left) having transferred weight on beat 1. Feet slightly apart, in close hold. **Cuban Motion is used throughout.**

## MAN

| Step | Description | Rhythm | Beat |
|---|---|---|---|
| 1 | LF forward | Q | 2 |
| 2 | Replace weight to RF | Q | 3 |
| 3 | LF to side and slightly back, pressure on the inside edge of the ball of the foot. Lower heel of LF and hips continue to move to left side on count 1 completing transfer of weight | S | 4,1 |
| 4 | RF back | Q | 2 |
| 5 | Replace weight to LF | Q | 3 |
| 6 | RF to side and slightly forward, pressure on the inside edge of the ball of the foot. | S | 4 |

2 bars

## LADY

| Step | Description | Rhythm | Beat |
|---|---|---|---|
| 1 | RF backward | Q | 2 |
| 2 | Replace weight to LF | Q | 3 |
| 3 | RF to side and slightly forward, pressure on the inside edge of the ball of the foot. Lower heel of RF and hips continue to move to right side on count 1 completing transfer of weight | S | 4,1 |
| 4 | LF forward | Q | 2 |
| 5 | Replace weight to RF | Q | 3 |
| 6 | LF to side and slightly back, pressure on the inside edge of the ball of the foot. | S | 4 |

2 bars

## 2  CUCARACHAS

Cucarachas, also known in the USA as Second Position Breaks, when danced in Mambo are usually danced in close hold. Start with the man's weight on RF (hip to right) and the lady's weight on LF (hip to left) having transferred weight on beat 1. Feet slightly apart, in close hold. **Cuban Motion is used throughout.**

## MAN

| Step | Description | Rhythm | Beat |
|------|-------------|--------|------|
| 1 | LF to side on inside edge of ball of foot, transfer part weight keeping heel of RF on the floor | Q | 2 |
| 2 | Replace weight to RF | Q | 3 |
| 3 | Close LF to RF and transfer weight to LF | S | 4,1 |
| 4 | RF to side with part weight keeping heel of LF on the floor | Q | 2 |
| 5 | Replace weight to LF | Q | 3 |
| 6 | Close RF to LF | S | 4 |
| | | | 2 bars |

## LADY

| Step | Description | Rhythm | Beat |
|------|-------------|--------|------|
| 1 | RF to side on inside edge of ball of foot, transfer part weight keeping heel of LF on the floor | Q | 2 |
| 2 | Replace weight to LF | Q | 3 |
| 3 | Close RF to LF and transfer weight to RF | S | 4,1 |
| 4 | LF to side with part weight keeping heel of RF on the floor | Q | 2 |
| 5 | Replace weight to RF | Q | 3 |
| 6 | Close LF to RF | S | 4 |
| | | | 2 bars |

Cucarachas are a crucial action to learn as they form the cornerstone of many Mambo figures. It is vital that on the "Slow" count the hip does not transfer until beat 1.

# 3   SHOULDER TO SHOULDER

This step is usually danced in close hold. Start with the man's weight on RF (hip to right) and the lady's weight on LF (hip to left) having transferred weight on beat 1. Feet slightly apart, in close hold. **Cuban Motion is used throughout.**

## MAN

| Step | Description | Rhythm | Beat |
|------|-------------|--------|------|
| 1-6 | Basic Movement | Q,Q,S | 2,3,4,1 |
|  |  | Q,Q,S | 2,3,4,1 |
| 7 | LF forward outside lady's left side | Q | 2 |
| 8 | Replace weight to RF | Q | 3 |
| 9 | LF to side | S | 4,1 |
| 10 | RF forward outside lady's right side | Q | 2 |
| 11 | Replace weight to LF | Q | 3 |
| 12 | RF to side | S | 4,1 |
| 13-18 | Repeat steps 7-12 | Q,Q,S | 2,3,4,1 |
|  |  | Q,Q,S | 2,3,4,1 |
| 19-24 | Basic Movement | Q,Q,S | 2,3,4,1 |
|  |  | Q,Q,S | 2,3,4,1 |
|  |  |  | 8 bars |

## LADY

| Step | Description | Rhythm | Beat |
|------|-------------|--------|------|
| 1-6 | Basic Movement | Q,Q,S | 2,3,4,1 |
|  |  | Q,Q,S | 2,3,4,1 |
| 7 | RF back in opening out position | Q | 2 |
| 8 | Replace weight to LF | Q | 3 |
| 9 | RF to side | S | 4,1 |
| 10 | LF back in opening out position | Q | 2 |
| 11 | Replace weight to RF | Q | 3 |
| 12 | LF to side | S | 4,1 |
| 13-18 | Repeat steps 7-12 | Q,Q,S | 2,3,4,1 |
|  |  | Q,Q,S | 2,3,4,1 |
| 19-24 | Basic Movement | Q,Q,S | 2,3,4,1 |
|  |  | Q,Q,S | 2,3,4,1 |
|  |  |  | 8 bars |

## 4   DOUBLE OPENING OUTS

Double Opening Outs is also known as Hand to Hand and in the USA as Fifth Position Breaks.

Start with the man's weight on RF (hip to right) and the lady's weight on LF (hip to left) having transferred weight on beat 1. Feet slightly apart, in close hold.

**Cuban Motion is used throughout.**

## MAN

| Step | Description | Rhythm | Beat |
|------|-------------|--------|------|
| 1-6 | Basic Movement | Q,Q,S | 2,3,4,1 |
|  |  | Q,Q,S | 2,3,4,1 |
| 7 | LF back in opening out position making up to ¼ turn to L | Q | 2 |
| 8 | Replace weight to RF in PP | Q | 3 |
| 9 | LF to side turning back to face lady passing through close hold | S | 4,1 |
| 10 | RF back in opening out position making up to ⁵/₈ turn to R releasing hold with right hand only | Q | 2 |
| 11 | Replace weight to LF in left side-by-side position | Q | 3 |
| 12 | RF to side turning back to face lady retaking close hold | S | 4,1 |
| 13-18 | Repeat steps 7-12 | Q,Q,S | 2,3,4,1 |
|  |  | Q,Q,S | 2,3,4,1 |
| 19-24 | Basic Movement | Q,Q,S | 2,3,4,1 |
|  |  | Q,Q,S | 2,3,4,1 |
|  |  |  | 8 bars |

# DOUBLE OPENING OUTS (cont.)

## LADY

| Step | Description | Rhythm | Beat |
|------|-------------|--------|------|
| 1-6 | Basic Movement | Q,Q,S | 2,3,4,1 |
|      |            | Q,Q,S | 2,3,4,1 |
| 7 | RF back in opening out position making up to ¼ turn to R | Q | 2 |
| 8 | Replace weight to LF in PP | Q | 3 |
| 9 | RF to side turning back to face man passing through close hold | S | 4,1 |
| 10 | LF back in opening out position making up to $5/8$ turn to L releasing hold with left hand only | Q | 2 |
| 11 | Replace weight to RF in left side-by-side position | Q | 3 |
| 12 | LF to side turning back to face man retaking close hold | S | 4,1 |
| 13-18 | Repeat steps 7-12 | Q,Q,S | 2,3,4,1 |
|       |              | Q,Q,S | 2,3,4,1 |
| 19-24 | Basic Movement | Q,Q,S | 2,3,4,1 |
|       |              | Q,Q,S | 2,3,4,1 |
|       |              |       | 8 bars |

It is very useful to learn the Shoulder to Shoulder and the Double Opening Outs together as the elements contained in both steps show the "opening out" type movement first of all for the lady and then the man.

The suggestion of releasing hold with one hand only and retaining hold with the man's left and the lady's right hands in the Double Opening Outs makes the step easier to learn, although when more advanced the student may wish to use hand to hand hold which should still, however, be kept tight and intimate.

Left: **Double Opening Outs, step 7**
Below: **Double Opening Outs, step 1O**

*Double Opening Outs are common in Mambo and Salsa and are often danced in waist-to-waist hold, particularly in Salsa.*

# 5    NEW YORK BREAK

New York Break, also known as New York and in the USA as Crossover Break, commences in close hold and progresses to open hold. It is important for club styling for both dancers to face each other whilst passing through the positions in between the "break steps" on either side.

Start with the man's weight on RF (hip to right) and the lady's weight on LF (hip to left) having transferred weight on beat 1. Feet slightly apart, in close hold. **Cuban Motion is used throughout.**

## MAN

| Step | Description | Rhythm | Beat |
|------|-------------|--------|------|
| 1-6 | Basic Movement | Q,Q,S | 2,3,4,1 |
|  |  | Q,Q,S | 2,3,4,1 |
| 7 | LF forward toe turned out in left side-by-side position making up to ¼ turn to R and releasing hold with right hand, inside hands joined | Q | 2 |
| 8 | Replace weight to RF, commence to turn L | Q | 3 |
| 9 | LF to side making up to ¼ turn to L between steps 8 & 9 taking hold of lady's left hand | S | 4,1 |
| 10 | RF forward toe turned out in right side-by-side position making up to ¼ turn to L, releasing lady's right hand, inside hands joined | Q | 2 |
| 11 | Replace weight to LF, commence to turn R | Q | 3 |
| 12 | RF to side making up to ¼ turn to R between steps 11 & 12 taking hold of lady's right hand | S | 4,1 |
| 13-18 | Repeat steps 7-12 | Q,Q,S | 2,3,4,1 |
|  |  | Q,Q,S | 2,3,4,1 |
| 19-24 | Basic Movement retaking close hold | Q,Q,S | 2,3,4,1 |
|  |  | Q,Q,S | 2,3,4,1 |
|  |  |  | 8 bars |

# NEW YORK BREAK (cont.)

## LADY

| Step | Description | Rhythm | Beat |
|------|-------------|--------|------|
| 1-6 | Basic Movement | Q,Q,S | 2,3,4,1 |
| | | Q,Q,S | 2,3,4,1 |
| 7 | RF forward toe turned out in right side-by-side position making up to ¼ turn to L, releasing hold with left hand, inside hands joined | Q | 2 |
| 8 | Replace weight to LF, commence to turn R | Q | 3 |
| 9 | RF to side making up to ¼ turn between steps 8 & 9 taking hold of man's right hand | S | 4,1 |
| 10 | LF forward toe turned out in left side-by-side position making up to ¼ turn to R, releasing man's left hand, inside hands joined | Q | 2 |
| 11 | Replace weight to RF, commence to turn L | Q | 3 |
| 12 | LF to side making up ¼ turn to L taking hold of man's left hand | S | 4,1 |
| 13-18 | Repeat steps 7-12 | Q,Q,S | 2,3,4,1 |
| | | Q,Q,S | 2,3,4,1 |
| 19-24 | Basic Movement retaking close hold | Q,Q,S | 2,3,4,1 |
| | | Q,Q,S | 2,3,4,1 |
| | | | 8 bars |

In club style Latin dancing, all open figures are danced with a tighter, more intimate feel than in competition style Latin. The New York Break is a good example of a step common to both styles in which it is vital to maintain Cuban motion and for the dancers to focus on each other. When the man leads this step the joined inside hands should be kept low and the dancers should not be too far apart, i.e. not at arm's length.

# CHA CHA CHA

**Time siganture:** 4/4 time. **Tempo:** 28 - 36 bpm. **FW:** ball flat throughout.

Readers may be surprised to find the Cha Cha Cha in a book about Salsa however, the Cha Cha Cha sound, derived from the Danzon, is officially recognised by the Cuban Government as being "created" by Enrique Jorrin, a Danzon composer and violinist who was awarded the Felix Varela Medal for his work. It was developed by the Cuban Charangas and became massively popular in Cuba in 1953. The authentic Cuban Cha Cha Cha contains a remarkable balance of sensuality and elegance and has a different sound from the style of Cha Cha Cha played by Salsa bands.

There is often a mistaken belief that the Cha Cha Cha is a musical descendant of the Mambo. This is because it chronologically followed the Mambo in the USA and was played mambo-style by the big Latin bands of the 1950s. It became popular with the greater American public due to its catchy rhythm which gave rise to the dance step from which the Cha Cha Cha got its name.

The Cha Cha Cha infiltrated mainstream music so extensively that it became a parody of itself and for a time became simply a novelty number. Fortunately, Cuban bands have maintained a passion for the Cha Cha Cha and have continued to present it as part of their programmes. Consequently, Salsa clubs, particularly authentic Cuban clubs, will sometimes play Cha Cha Cha.

Club style Cha Cha Cha is danced in a more sensual manner than its "International" competition style counterpart and has been chosen as the fourth dance in this book because it also has been standardised with "off beat" timing which can be difficult for social dancers. As with Mambo, it is also common to see the "break" step danced on the first beat of the bar rather than on beat two, which is generally accepted as being correct. The basic figures in this book are Cha Cha Cha steps that will simply introduce the Salsero to a graceful and traditional dance form.

The club style Cha Cha Cha is a spot dance and an in-depth understanding of Cuban Motion is required. It is usually danced in close hold.

# CHA CHA CHA

---

ALTHOUGH THESE FIRST FIVE BASIC CHA CHA CHA
STEPS ARE SHOWN WITH THE "BREAK" STEP
ON COUNT 2, IN CLUBS IT IS OFTEN
DANCED ON COUNT 1.

---

# 1   THE BASIC MOVEMENT IN PLACE

This step amounts to "step, step, Cha Cha Cha!" It can be danced in close hold and separately. Start with the man's weight on RF (hip to right) and lady's weight on LF (hip to left) feet slightly apart. **Cuban Motion is used throughout.**

## MAN

| Step | Description | Rhythm | Beat |
|------|-------------|--------|------|
| 1 | LF step in place, transfer weight to LF | Q | 2 |
| 2 | RF step in place, transfer weight to RF | Q | 3 |
| 3 | LF to side, small step | ½ | 4 |
| 4 | RF moves towards LF, small step | ½ | & |
| 5 | LF to side, small step | Q | 1 |
| 6 | RF step in place, transfer weight to RF | Q | 2 |
| 7 | LF step in place, transfer weight to LF | Q | 3 |
| 8 | RF to side, small step | ½ | 4 |
| 9 | LF moves towards RF, small step | ½ | & |
| 10 | RF to side, small step | Q | 1 |

2 bars

## LADY

| Step | Description | Rhythm | Beat |
|------|-------------|--------|------|
| 1 | RF step in place, transfer weight to RF | Q | 2 |
| 2 | LF step in place, transfer weight to LF | Q | 3 |
| 3 | RF to side, small step | ½ | 4 |
| 4 | LF moves towards RF, small step | ½ | & |
| 5 | RF to side, small step | Q | 1 |
| 6 | LF step in place, transfer weight to LF | Q | 2 |
| 7 | RF step in place, transfer weight to RF | Q | 3 |
| 8 | LF to side, small step | ½ | 4 |
| 9 | RF moves towards LF, small step | ½ | & |
| 10 | LF to side, small step | Q | 1 |

2 bars

Steps 3,4&5 and 8,9&10 (counts 4&1 of each bar) are known as the Cha Cha Cha Chassé or Triple Step. This is a useful way of practising the rhythm.

## 2 THE BASIC MOVEMENT

The Basic Movement is usually danced in close hold. It can also be danced separately and progressively forwards and backwards.

Start with the man's weight on RF (hip to right) and lady's weight on LF (hip to left) feet slightly apart.

**Cuban Motion is used throughout.**

## MAN

| Step | Description | Rhythm | Beat |
|------|-------------|--------|------|
| 1 | LF forward | Q | 2 |
| 2 | Replace weight to RF | Q | 3 |
| 3,4,5 | LF to side to Chassé (LF, RF, LF) | ½,½,Q | 4&1 |
| 6 | RF back | Q | 2 |
| 7 | Replace weight to LF | Q | 3 |
| 8,9,10 | RF to side to Chassé (RF, LF, RF) | ½,½,Q | 4&1 |
| | | | 2 bars |

## LADY

| Step | Description | Rhythm | Beat |
|------|-------------|--------|------|
| 1 | RF back | Q | 2 |
| 2 | Replace weight to LF | Q | 3 |
| 3,4,5 | RF to side to Chassé (RF, LF, RF) | ½,½,Q | 4&1 |
| 6 | LF forward | Q | 2 |
| 7 | Replace weight to RF | Q | 3 |
| 8,9,10 | LF to side to Chassé (LF, RF, LF) | ½,½,Q | 4&1 |
| | | | 2 bars |

The Basic Movement of the Cha Cha Cha in Club style Latin dancing is kept very earthy and intimate and should have a more easy, sexy appearance than the competition style Cha Cha.

## 3  SHOULDER TO SHOULDER

The Shoulder to Shoulder is usually danced in close hold.

Start with the man's weight on RF (hip to right) and lady's weight on LF (hip to left) feet slightly apart.

**Cuban Motion is used throughout.**

## MAN

| Step | Description | Rhythm | Beat |
|------|-------------|--------|------|
| 1-10 | Basic Movement | Q,Q,½,½,Q | 2,3,4&1 |
|      |                | Q,Q,½,½,Q | 2,3,4&1 |
| 11 | LF forward outside lady's left side | Q | 2 |
| 12 | Replace weight to RF | Q | 3 |
| 13,14,15 | LF to side to Chassé (LF, RF, LF) | ½,½,Q | 4&1 |
| 16 | RF forward outside lady's right side | Q | 2 |
| 17 | Replace weight to LF | Q | 3 |
| 18,19,20 | RF to side to Chassé (RF, LF, RF) | ½,½,Q | 4&1 |
| 21-30 | Repeat steps 11-20 | Q,Q,½,½,Q | 2,3,4&1 |
|       |                    | Q,Q,½,½,Q | 2,3,4&1 |
| 31-40 | Basic Movement | Q,Q,½,½,Q | 2,3,4&1 |
|       |                | Q,Q,½,½,Q | 2,3,4&1 |
|       |                |           | 8 bars |

## SHOULDER TO SHOULDER (cont.)

| Step | Description | Rhythm | Beat |
|------|-------------|--------|------|
| 1-10 | Basic Movement | Q,Q,½,½,Q | 2,3,4&1 |
| | | Q,Q,½,½,Q | 2,3,4&1 |
| 11 | RF back in opening out position | Q | 2 |
| 12 | Replace weight to LF | Q | 3 |
| 13,14,15 | RF to side to Chassé (RF, LF, RF) | ½,½,Q | 4&1 |
| 16 | LF back in opening out position | Q | 2 |
| 17 | Replace weight to RF | Q | 3 |
| 18,19,20 | LF to side to Chassé (LF, RF, LF) | ½,½,Q | 4&1 |
| 21-30 | Repeat steps 11-20 | Q,Q,½,½,Q | 2,3,4&1 |
| | | Q,Q,½,½,Q | 2,3,4&1 |
| 31-40 | Basic Movement | Q,Q,½,½,Q | 2,3,4&1 |
| | | Q,Q,½,½,Q | 2,3,4&1 |
| | | | 8 bars |

***Shoulder to shoulder**: on this step, the focus of attention for the man should always be the lady - as ever!*

# 4 DOUBLE OPENING OUTS

Double Opening Outs is also known internationally as Hand to Hand and in the USA as Fifth Position Breaks.

Start with the man's weight on RF (hip to right) and lady's weight on LF (hip to left) feet slightly apart.

**Cuban Motion is used throughout.**

## MAN

| Step | Description | Rhythm | Beat |
|------|-------------|--------|------|
| 1-10 | Basic Movement | Q,Q,½,½,Q | 2,3,4&1 |
| | | Q,Q,½,½,Q | 2,3,4&1 |
| 11 | LF back in opening out position making up to ¼ turn to L | Q | 2 |
| 12 | Replace weight to RF in PP | Q | 3 |
| 13,14,15 | LF to side to Chassé (LF, RF, LF) turning back to face lady passing through close hold | ½,½,Q | 4&1 |
| 16 | RF back in opening out position making up to ⅝ turn to R releasing hold with right hand only | Q | 2 |
| 17 | Replace weight to LF in left side-by-side position | Q | 3 |
| 18,19,20 | RF to side to Chassé (RF, LF, RF) turning back to face lady retaking close hold | ½,½,Q | 4&1 |
| 21-30 | Repeat steps 11-20 | Q,Q,½,½,Q | 2,3,4&1 |
| | | Q,Q,½,½,Q | 2,3,4&1 |
| 31-40 | Basic Movement | Q,Q,½,½,Q | 2,3,4&1 |
| | | Q,Q,½,½,Q | 2,3,4&1 |
| | | | 8 bars |

## DOUBLE OPENING OUTS (cont.)

### LADY

| Step | Description | Rhythm | Beat |
|------|-------------|--------|------|
| 1-10 | Basic Movement | Q,Q,½,½,Q | 2,3,4&1 |
|      |              | Q,Q,½,½,Q | 2,3,4&1 |
| 11 | RF back in opening out position making up to ¼ turn to R | Q | 2 |
| 12 | Replace weight to LF in PP | Q | 3 |
| 13,14,15 | RF to side to Chassé (RF, LF, RF) turning back to face man passing through close hold | ½,½,Q | 4&1 |
| 16 | LF back in opening out position making up to ⅝ turn to L releasing hold with left hand only | Q | 2 |
| 17 | Replace weight to RF in left side-by-side position | Q | 3 |
| 18,19,20 | LF to side to Chassé (LF, RF, LF) turning back to face man retaking close hold | ½,½,Q | 4&1 |
| 21-30 | Repeat steps 11-20 | Q,Q,½,½,Q | 2,3,4&1 |
|       |                    | Q,Q,½,½,Q | 2,3,4&1 |
| 31-40 | Basic Movement | Q,Q,½,½,Q | 2,3,4&1 |
|       |                | Q,Q,½,½,Q | 2,3,4&1 |
|       |                |           | 8 bars |

As in the Mambo, it is very useful to learn the Shoulder to Shoulder and the Double Opening Outs together as the elements contained in both steps show the "opening out" type movement first of all for the lady and then the man. The suggestion of releasing hold with one hand only and retaining hold with the man's left and the lady's right hands in the Double Opening Outs makes the step easier to learn, although when more advanced the student may wish to use hand to hand hold which should still, however, be kept tight and intimate.

## 5   NEW YORK BREAK

New York Break, also known as New York and Crossover Break, commences in close hold and progresses to open hold. It is important for club styling for both dancers to face each other whilst dancing the Cha Cha Cha Chassé in between the "break steps" on either side.

Start with the man's weight on RF (hip to right) and lady's weight on LF (hip to left) feet slightly apart.

**Cuban Motion is used throughout.**

## MAN

| Step | Description | Rhythm | Beat |
|------|-------------|--------|------|
| 1-10 | Basic Movement | Q,Q,½,½,Q | 2,3,4&1 |
|      |              | Q,Q,½,½,Q | 2,3,4&1 |
| 11 | LF forward toe turned out in left side-by-side position making up to ¼ turn to R and releasing hold with right hand, inside hands joined | Q | 2 |
| 12 | Replace weight to RF, commence to turn L | Q | 3 |
| 13,14,15 | LF to side to Chassé (LF, RF, LF) making up to ¼ turn to L between steps 12 & 15 taking hold of lady's left hand | ½,½,Q | 4&1 |
| 16 | RF forward toe turned out in right side-by-side position making up to ¼ turn to L, releasing lady's right hand, inside hands joined | Q | 2 |
| 17 | Replace weight to LF, commence to turn R | Q | 3 |
| 18,19,20 | RF to side to Chassé (RF, LF, RF) making up to ¼ turn to R between steps 17 & 20 taking hold of lady's right hand | ½,½,Q | 4&1 |

## NEW YORK BREAK (cont.)

| Step | Description | Rhythm | Beat |
|------|-------------|--------|------|
| 21-30 | Repeat steps 11-20 | Q,Q,½,½,Q | 2,3,4&1 |
| | | Q,Q,½,½,Q | 2,3,4&1 |
| 31-40 | Basic Movement retaking close hold | Q,Q,½,½,Q | 2,3,4&1 |
| | | Q,Q,½,½,Q | 2,3,4&1 |
| | | | 8 bars |

## LADY

| Step | Description | Rhythm | Beat |
|------|-------------|--------|------|
| 1-10 | Basic Movement | Q,Q,½,½,Q | 2,3,4&1 |
| | | Q,Q,½,½,Q | 2,3,4&1 |
| 11 | RF forward toe turned out in left side-by-side position making up to ¼ turn to L and releasing hold with right hand, inside hands joined | Q | 2 |
| 12 | Replace weight to LF, commence to turn R | Q | 3 |
| 13,14,15 | RF to side to Chassé (RF, LF, RF) making up to ¼ turn to R between steps 12 & 15 taking hold of man's right hand | ½,½,Q | 4&1 |
| 16 | LF forward toe turned out in right side-by-side position making up to ¼ turn to R, releasing man's right hand, inside hands joined | Q | 2 |
| 17 | Replace weight to RF, commence to turn L | Q | 3 |
| 18,19,20 | LF to side to Chassé (LF, RF, LF) making up to ¼ turn to L between steps 17 & 20 taking hold of man's left hand | ½,½,Q | 4&1 |

## NEW YORK BREAK (cont.)

| Step | Description | Rhythm | Beat |
|------|-------------|--------|------|
| 21-30 | Repeat steps 11-20 | Q,Q,½,½,Q | 2,3,4&1 |
| | | Q,Q,½,½,Q | 2,3,4&1 |
| 31-40 | Basic Movement retaking close hold | Q,Q,½,½,Q | 2,3,4&1 |
| | | Q,Q,½,½,Q | 2,3,4&1 |
| | | | 8 bars |

As in Mambo it is vital to maintain Cuban motion and for the dancers to focus on each other. When the man leads this step the joined inside hands should be kept low and the dancers should not be too far apart, i.e. not at arm's length.

"REMEMBER: THE AIM IS NOT TO MAKE EASY MOVES LOOK DIFFICULT BUT TO MAKE DIFFICULT MOVES LOOK EASY – PRACTICE MAKES PERFECT."

# SALSA & MERENGUE ESSENTIAL INFORMATION

This section includes a glossary of terms used in the Latino dance scene, lists of films, books, contact addresses and telephone numbers of where you can obtain club listings. Plus information on how to find both current and prospective qualified instructors.

In short, everything you need to know about Salsa and Merengue!

# Glossary of Latin Terms

### AGOGÓ
A West African percussion instrument introduced by Brazilian musicians.

### BARRIO, EL
The name initially coined to describe the districts housing large numbers of Latin-American immigrants.

### BOLERO
The Cuban Bolero, at its slowest and most sentimental, is a romantic Latin-American ballad sometimes covered by Salsa bands. Bolero music is used for the dance called the Rumba in "International" style Latin-American competitions worldwide. This is because when Rumba was first introduced to the West it was largely danced to Son music. As the tempo for competitions became slower, the music of Son was no longer appropriate and eventually the tempo became so slow that Bolero music was used.

### BONGO
The bongo is a small double drum usually played by seated musicians in most Cuban music and extensively in Salsa. Its heads are tuned a fourth apart.

### BOSSA NOVA
Largely distinct from Salsa, the Bossa Nova is currently also enjoying a revival in the "easy listening" scene. It is a fusion of Brazilian rhythm and cool jazz.

### CHARANGA
A form of orchestra with a front line of flutes and violins especially known for playing Danzon and Cha Cha Cha.

### CLAVE
The rhythmic pattern which is the basis of all Cuban music.

### CLAVES
Two round wooden sticks struck together in which the claves player plays the relevant clave pattern.

## CONGA DRUM
An important instrument in Salsa of which there are several types, including "quinto", "conga" and "tumbadora".

## CONGA RHYTHM
One of the more simple Cuban rhythms, originally a carnival dance march.

## CONGUERO
A conga player.

## CONJUNTO
A form of orchestra with full Latin percussion section and a front line of trumpets, especially known for playing Son.

## CONTRADANZA
The 17th century French dance from which the Danzon was derived.

## DANZON
A Cuban ballroom dance with European influence played by charangas.

## GUAJIRA
A musical form often describing Cuban country life, the most famous probably being Guantanamera.

## GUARACHA
A Cuban musical form commonly used by Salsa bands.

## GÜIRO
A musical instrument held in one hand and scraped with a stick.

## HABANERA
A Cuban dance originally from Spain which along with the Milonga is a fore-runner of the Tango.

## LATIN JAZZ
Afro-Cuban rhythm fused with jazz.

## LATIN ROCK
Afro-Cuban rhythm fused with rock.

## MARACCAS
A small, tuned musical instrument comprising a pair of rattles filled with seeds and shaken.

## MAXIXE
A ballroom dance from Brazil.

## MONTUNO
Developed by the Conjunto Orchestras, a Montuno Section in a musical arrangement is where the rhythm takes over the melody, often used for improvisation in Salsa.

## ORQUESTA TIPICA
A way of describing a typical Cuban orchestra.

## PACHANGA
A Latin-American rhythm which enjoyed brief popularity in America during the early 1960s.

## RUMBA
When the Rumba first became popular in the West during the 1930s almost all "Rumbas" were, in fact, Sons. The Cuban Rumba is a traditional dance with a complex heritage and is largely divided into three forms: Rumba Yambu, Rumba Guaguancó and Rumba Columbia. The music for the dance called Rumba for International Latin-American competitions is usually Bolero. A Rumba can also be a gathering in which Cuban music and dance is celebrated.

## SALSERO
A person who enjoys Salsa music and dance.

## SAMBA
A Brazilian dance and musical form.

### SEPTETO/SEXTETO
Forms of Cuban orchestras very popular during the 1930s.

### SON
Cuban dance music with equal African and Spanish elements of which the most famous is probably El Manicero (The Peanut Vendor).

### SON MONTUNO
A form of Cuban music.

### SONERO
A player or singer of Sons sometimes used to describe lead singers in Salsa.

### TANGO
An Argentinian dance deriving from the Milonga and the Cuban Habanera.

### TIMBALES
Cylindrical drums on a tripod played with sticks, often with the addition of cowbells and a cymbal.

### TRES
A nine-stringed Cuban guitar used extensively by Conjuntos.

### ZAPATEO
A Spanish-influenced Cuban country dance.

# Bibliography

*Rumba - Dance and Social Change in Contemporary Cuba* – Yvonne Daniel
*The Latin Tinge* – John Storm Roberts
*Black Music of Two Worlds* – John Storm Roberts
*Music of Latin America* – Nicholas Slonimsky
*Salsa!* – Hernando Calvo Ospina
*Samba* – Alma Guillermoprieto
*Tango and the Political Economy of Passion* – Marta E Soviliano
*Tango* – Collier, Cooper, Azzi, Martin
*The Authentic Latin-American Dances* – Margot Sampson
*Latin & American Dances* – Doris Lavelle
*The Technique of Latin Dancing* – Walter Laird
*The Revised Technique of Latin-American Dancing* – ISTD
*The Ballroom Technique* - ISTD
*The Technique of Ballroom Dancing* – Guy Howard
*Modern Ballroom Dancing* (Various Editions) – Victor Sylvester
*Social Dances of the 19th Century* – P J Richardson
*Tango Argentino, The Technique* – Paul Bottomer
*How To Be A Good Dancer* – Arthur Murray
*The Fred Astaire Dance Book* – Fred Astaire Organisation
*The Principles of Classical Dance* – Anthony Dowell

# Filmography

What's Cuba Playing At?
The Afro Cuban All Stars - Salon of Dreams
The Rumba Rage
Salsa – The Movie
Strictly Salsa – Elder Sanchez
Sensual Salsa – Elder Sanchez
Latin-American Rhythms – Elder Sanchez
The Mambo Kings
Dirty Dancing
Dollar Mambo
Lambada – The Movie
Tango Bar
Tango – Les Exiles de Gardel
Naked Tango
The Tango Lesson
Bolero
Rumba
Flying Down to Rio
Weekend in Havana
That Night in Rio

# Useful Addresses

The following organisations will be happy to help find your nearest qualified instructor in Merengue and Salsa.

**UNITED KINGDOM ALLIANCE LTD**
Centenary House
38/40 Station Road
BLACKPOOL
FY4 1EU

Tel: 01253 408828
Fax: 01253 408066
(Contact Paul Harris through United Kingdom Alliance)

**BRITISH DANCE COUNCIL**
Terpsichore House
240 Merton Road
South Wimbledon
LONDON
SW19 1EQ

Tel:    0181 545 0085
Fax:    0181 545 0225

**CENTRAL COUNCIL OF PHYSICAL RECREATION**
Francis House
Francis Street
London
SW1P 1DE

Tel:    0171 828 3163
Fax:    0171 630 8820

# How To Find Out More About Your Local Salsa Scene

**SALSA WORLD**
PO Box 406
HORSHAM
West Sussex RH12 1BR

For hot dance tips, news, reviews and listing get the Salsa magazine, *Salsa World*.

**SALSA Pa'Ti**
PO Box 2098
Chigwell Road
CHIGWELL
Essex IG7 4BG
E-mail: salsapa21@aol.com    Hotline: 07071 880733

The free bimonthly newsletter and mail-order company for the latest, hottest and spiciest new releases of Salsa, Merengue, Cumbia, Latin Jazz and much, much, more!

**LATIN LONDON MAGAZINE**
Latinzone Enterprises Ltd
PO Box 13338
LONDON W8 7ZY

The bi-monthly guide to London's red-hot Latin scene – music, events, reviews, travel and more!

**THE SALSAMANIAC**
Salsamania
117 Kingsbrook Road
Chorlton
Manchester M16 8NY
Tel & Fax: 0161 860 5713

The fanzine for Latin music lovers in the North.

# Professional Teachers' Diploma

The following requirements are for any teachers using this book as a guide to study for a Club Dance Division Professional Teachers' Diploma in Merengue and Salsa with the United Kingdom Alliance of Professional Teachers of Dancing.

## 1 DEMONSTRATION

Candidates will be required to give a thorough demonstration both as man and lady of the professional syllabus figures which is more extensive than in this book. They may also be asked to dance solo.

## 2 HISTORY

A thorough knowledge of the history of Salsa, both the music and the dance, is required. Questions on related dances may be asked.

## 3 THEORY

Candidates must be able to describe in detail both man's and lady's steps of patterns selected by the examiner. They must have a clear understanding of all terms used in Terminology and be able to describe all holds. The ability to count in beats and bars and a knowledge of the tempo played for Merengue and Salsa in clubs is required.

## 4 ABILITY TO TEACH

Candidates will be required to answer questions relating to both the teaching of class work and private lessons and identifying common faults. Candidates already conducting a class will also be examined on a vocational basis at their place of work.

## 5 BEYOND THE SYLLABUS

The candidate may show an improvised version of their own approach to Merengue and Salsa, including more complicated variations, and explain any differences from the recommended syllabus style.

# Acknowledgements

In a career that has been dictated by dance since 1968 I have been lucky in that there have been several people at the top of their fields who have influenced my thinking and contributed to my conclusions at this point in time.

Derek Young, one of the greatest ever exponents of Old Time dancing, was my first competitive teacher and guided me through a hugely successful Juvenile career with great care before passing me on to the late Major Eric Hancox, who introduced me to principles of both Ballroom and authentic Latin-American dancing that remain to this day.

As an adult Latin-American champion I learned first hand from the late Doris Lavelle about the introduction of the Latin-American dances in the West and shared with my other coaches, Sydney Francis, Michael Stylianos and in particular the renowned Walter Laird, a common interest in furthering the use of authentic music in International-style Latin-American competitions, a battle which Walter still fights today.

John Delroy initiated my interest in Showdance and Theatre Arts and began a progression which encouraged me to enter drama school where authenticity to the character and artistic truth are, of course, paramount. I was fortunate enough to have an acting coach from the Moscow Arts Theatre who was a great believer in the work of Stanislavsky, along with Ballet, Jazz and Historical dance teachers who fully understood the necessity to strive for authenticity in performance.

Finally, my work at the Actors Centre has brought about an association with Isabelle Fokine, Artistic Director of the Fokine Estate Archive and granddaughter of the legendary Russian choreographer Michel Fokine, one of the most influential figures in the history of dance. Miss Fokine has danced with the Bolshoi Ballet, the Kirov Ballet and the American Ballet Theatre, and I could wish for no greater benchmark to cement my beliefs that the principles and dynamics of partnering are the same, regardless of whether it is high level ballet or club style social dancing.

# With Thanks

Richard Dudley

David Paton

Pineapple Agency

Big City Studios

Costume Studio

Kiyono Miyagi

David Roberts

Anna Luong

Julian Atlee

Ashley Green

Kirsten Wheeler

Joe Pritchard

May Kwan

Ruby Young

Jocelyn Young

Ishra

Robert Harkavy

THIS BOOK IS DEDICATED TO MY MOTHER AND TO MY LATE FATHER, THOMAS HARRIS, WHO WOULD BE PROUD AND VERY HAPPY THAT ALL HIS DRIVING WAS WORTHWHILE!

# MORE BOOKS & CDS FOR DANCING FEET!

## THE SOCIAL DANCE SURVIVAL GUIDE

"This book covers every aspect of together dancing, and it shows you clearly and plainly how to make that start into the fabulous world of dancing." *David Roberts: UKA and the British Dance Council*

Written by **Ken Akrill**, a widely-respected professional dance teacher and examiner, the book teaches the non-dancer the important, basic aspects of social ballroom and Latin dancing. The convenient chart form shows foot direction and postitioning – useful for anyone not able to see the steps demonstrated by a teacher.

Emphasis is placed on developing a sound basis in: Waltz and Foxtrot; traditional Latin American dances, and the increasingly-popular Club Latino dances: Merengue and Salsa. There's also a very useful section on dances that you can use at discos when the space is small and the pace is hectic!

*£6.95*

## LEARN TO DANCE: MODERN JIVE

This book & CD package is the only complete guide to Modern Jive - the fast and stylish partner dance also known as French-style Jive. It's a blend of jitterbug and rock 'n' roll that you can dance to music from fifties swing to today's chart hits!

There are over 50 moves and 12 complete routines to make you the star of the dance floor! The authors are Robert Austin and Claire Hilliard, from the highly successful leJIVE organisation.

*Book and CD: £10.95*

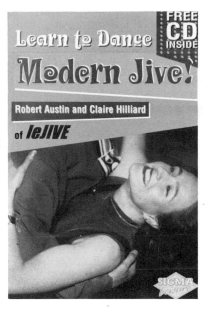

## START TO DANCE: MODERN JIVE

**Recommended by Le Roc**: the French Jive Chapter of the UKA professional dance teaching body. The 12-track CD has been specially engineered for jive dancing. It includes brand-new recordings from the gently-swinging "My Baby Just Cares For Me" to "Rhythm Is A Dancer" and "Just Can't Get Enough"! The booklet from the well-respected Le Roc organisation teaches you the basics of French Jive!

*£6.95*

## COUNTRY & WESTERN LINE DANCING FOR COWGIRLS & COWBOYS:
### Step-by-Step Instructions

***TOP VALUE BOOK & CD PACKAGE!***

This has been the number 1 best-selling line dance package in the UK since we launched it in 1996. Packed with 53 dances and supplied with a FREE CD. **Just £12.95 for the complete package -** that's 24 pence per dance plus the pleasure of a top-quality CD of authentic C&W music!

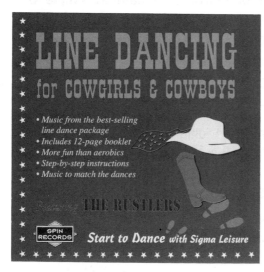

## SPECIAL OFFER FOR COUNTRY & WESTERN ENTHUSIASTS!

We also offer the CD from "COUNTRY & WESTERN LINE DANCING FOR COWGIRLS & COWBOYS" with a booklet of four popular line dances – ideal as an introduction to line dancing!

*£6.95*

## INTERNATIONAL LINE DANCE FAVORITES: Step-by-Step Instructions

**INTERNATIONAL LINE DANCE FAVORITES**

Judy Dygdon & Tony Conger

FEATURING MUSIC FROM

SCOOTER LEE
THE WORLD'S LEADING COUNTRY MUSIC DANCE ARTIST!

FREE CD INSIDE!

The follow-up to the fastest-selling line dancing package in the UK- "Line Dancing for Cowgirls & Cowboys"- this new book and CD is crammed full with clear, tried and tested instructions for all the current UK favourites. It also features many new dances making the total number up to an amazing 52!

Its unique system of step-by-step, beat-by-beat instructions, makes it suitable for both beginners and experienced dancers. You will be guided in a carefully graded progression from the more simple to the most challenging of routines.

**PLUS: FREE CD BY SCOOTER LEE - THE LEADING COUNTRY MUSIC DANCE ARTIST!**

*All for just £10.95 - Book & CD!*

Please add £2 p&p for UK orders. Additional charges may apply outside the UK. We welcome VISA & MASTERCARD. Orders to:

Sigma Leisure, 1 South Oak Lane, Wilmslow, Cheshire, SK9 6AR. Tel: 01625-531035;  Fax: 01625-536800

**Our complete on-line catalogue is on the Internet::**

http://www.sigmapress.co.uk